it the different ideas that
and for instance of Derek Jarman
for instance
and

August '14

news of the keep

in its smashes to

Tentative ideas for a
manifesto after 1 1/3 year at an
art school.

it is evident that the arts have
been ossified into respective
spheres unnaturally, dancing,
the opera house, the theatre,
architecture, the concert hall.
etc. probably the least
effective the art gallery, a
structure perfected in the C19.

Theatre ballet and painting
must be revived. This cannot
be achieved separately. There
must be intercommunication

The genuine participating
audience has been lost
lack of audience reaction
has been made a virtue.

Derek Jarman: A Portrait

Derek Jarman: A Portrait

with 151 illustrations, 90 in color

Introduction by Roger Wollen

with contributions by:
James Cary Parkes
Matt Cook
Christopher Lloyd
Stuart Morgan
Michael O'Pray
Peter Snow
Yolanda Sonnabend
Gray Watson

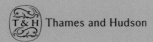 Thames and Hudson

BARBICAN ART GALLERY

Left: Jarman priming canvases, 1992
Endpapers: Drawings for 'Corfe Castle' film, 1975
Frontispiece: Jarman after completing *Dead Sexy*, May 1993

Any copy of this book issued by the publisher as a paperback is sold
subject to the condition that it shall not by way of trade or otherwise be
lent, resold, hired out or otherwise circulated without the publisher's prior
consent in any form of binding or cover other than that in which it is
published and without a similar condition including these words being
imposed on a subsequent purchaser.

© 1996 Thames and Hudson Ltd, London

All essays © the authors 1996; Chronology © Roger Wollen 1996.
Derek Jarman texts reprinted with the kind permission of the Estate
of Derek Jarman, Random House, Quartet Books, BFI Publications,
Afterimage, Faber and Faber; unpublished texts appear with the
permission of Peake Associates, London. Jarman's paintings and designs
© Estate of Derek Jarman

First published in the United States of America in 1996 by Thames
and Hudson Inc., 500 Fifth Avenue, New York, New York 10110
Library of Congress Catalog Card Number 96-60202
ISBN 0-500-01723-9
Printed and bound in Italy

Contents

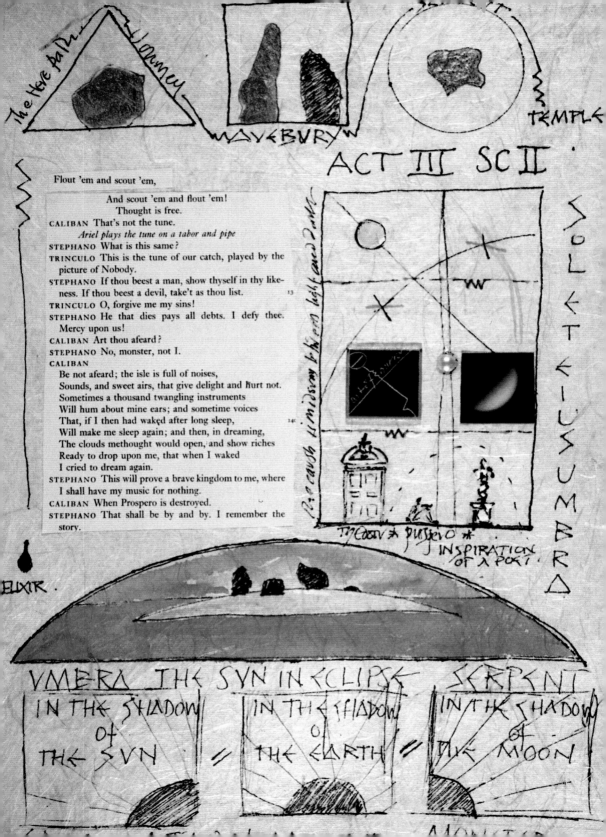

The Here path — Journey

MAVEBVRY

TEMPLE

ACT III SC II

SOL ET EIUS UMBRA

Flout 'em and scout 'em,

And scout 'em and flout 'em!
Thought is free.

CALIBAN That's not the tune.

Ariel plays the tune on a tabor and pipe

STEPHANO What is this same?

TRINCULO This is the tune of our catch, played by the
picture of Nobody.

STEPHANO If thou beest a man, show thyself in thy like-
ness. If thou beest a devil, take't as thou list.

TRINCULO O, forgive me my sins!

STEPHANO He that dies pays all debts. I defy thee.
Mercy upon us!

CALIBAN Art thou afeard?

STEPHANO No, monster, not I.

CALIBAN
Be not afeard; the isle is full of noises,
Sounds, and sweet airs, that give delight and hurt not.
Sometimes a thousand twangling instruments
Will hum about mine ears; and sometime voices
That, if I then had waked after long sleep,
Will make me sleep again; and then, in dreaming,
The clouds methought would open, and show riches
Ready to drop upon me, that when I waked
I cried to dream again.

STEPHANO This will prove a brave kingdom to me, where
I shall have my music for nothing.

CALIBAN When Prospero is destroyed.

STEPHANO That shall be by and by. I remember the
story.

ELIXIR.

INSPIRATION OF A POET

VMBRA THE SVN IN ECLIPSE SERPENT

IN THE SHADOW OF THE SVN

IN THE SHADOW OF THE EARTH

IN THE SHADOW OF THE MOON

Acknowledgments

This publication coincides with the 1996 exhibition *Derek Jarman: A Portrait* at the Barbican Art Gallery, London (9 May–18 August) and the Hatton Gallery at Newcastle University (7 September–8 October).

The exhibition had a complicated history. I was greatly impressed by Jarman's 1984 ICA show and when the opportunity arose to organize a major retrospective, as part of Visual Arts UK in the Northern Region in 1996, I contacted Jarman in early 1993 with the idea, seeking his agreement. Shortly afterwards the Hatton Gallery indicated its interest in presenting the exhibition and later still the Barbican Art Gallery joined the Hatton as joint organizer. Neither the exhibition nor the book would have come about without the support of Derek Jarman himself. The help, advice, and assistance provided by many of his family, friends and colleagues were equally important.

Keith Collins has provided invaluable support, as have Richard Salmon, Jarman's dealer from 1987, James Mackay, producer of most of Jarman's films since the early 1980s, and Tony Peake, Jarman's literary agent and biographer.

Particular mention must be made of Jarman's sister, Gaye Temple; his long-time friends Roger and Lindy Ford, Brenda Lukey, Christopher Hobbs, John Dewe-Matthews, Lady Anya Sainsbury, Peter Doherty, Neil Murray and Ray Dean, and his former teachers at Canford School, Robin Noscoe and Andrew Davis, as well as friends and colleagues Lynn Hanke, Peter Fillingham, Piers Clemett, Digby Green, Pia Goddard and Howard Sooley. I would like to thank Gaia Shaw, Maggy Taylor and Matthew Cook for lending me copies of their postgraduate studies of Jarman's work, all of which contained valuable insights, as did the projects undertaken by Charlotte and William Ford.

Janet Moat, Special Materials Librarian at the BFI Library, Patricia Methven of the King's College Archive, Archivist Stephen Chaplin at the Slade School of Art, Dr Jane Birkett at the Theatre Museum and Stella Halkyard at the Rylands Library in Manchester are all deserving of thanks for their support and assistance, as are Alan Haydon and James Bustard at Northern Arts in Newcastle upon Tyne, who supported the project in the early days.

The exhibition could not have been presented without the willing help of the many people who own paintings by Derek Jarman and who allowed access to their collections, provided hospitality and much invaluable information.

Special thanks are also due to the contributors to this volume: James Cary Parkes, Matthew Cook, Christopher Lloyd, Stuart Morgan, Michael O'Pray, Peter Snow, Yolanda Sonnabend and Gray Watson.

Finally my thanks to John Hoole and Conrad Bodman at the Barbican Art Gallery, Gavin Robson and Anthony Parton at the Hatton Gallery and my wife Sophia who has read my texts, visited many of Jarman's friends and collectors with me and provided much needed advice.

Roger Wollen
Exhibition researcher

FOLLOWING PAGES: Jarman painting a sphinx (possibly for *A Garden in Luxor*, 1972 and *The Art of Mirrors*, 1973)

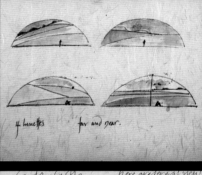
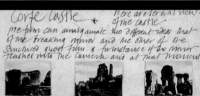

arman giving his impression of a chameleon, late 1992

Right: The censing of Jarman in the
Canonization of St Derek by the Sisters
of Perpetual Indulgence at Dungeness,
22 September 1991

Below: Jarman wearing plastic cape
with US dollar bills, October 1969
or before

Jarman holding his sculpture *Construction*, spring 1968

INTRODUCTION
Facets of Derek Jarman

Roger Wollen, researcher for the exhibition *Derek Jarman: A Portrait*, 1996

Painter, film-maker, writer and designer: Derek Jarman worked in a bewildering variety of media. Despite one's initial response that he couldn't be successful in all of them, it soon becomes clear that in each of these four careers, Jarman's achievements were considerable. How was that possible? He had talent and he had luck. But there were two other reasons: his use of a range of media to explore and present his ideas and the fact that he was very much his own man.

His output was not compartmentalized: he put over his ideas in every medium open to him. As a result the work has a consistency and coherence, not only at any one time, but across his life and output as a whole. Compare, for example, his feature films with his painting.[1] Few of his films are narrative works in the tradition of the commercial cinema; they are much more concerned with a flow of imagery, a series of two-dimensional compositions on screen, very much like paintings and collages. Where there is narrative it is often temporally disjointed and sophisticated, combining several time phases, viewpoints and character sets. In *Caravaggio* Jarman is dealing specifically with the life, work and the creative processes of a major artist, but other films also draw on the iconography of fine art.[2] At the same time Jarman created art works which are derived from and use iconography from the feature films (the 'GBH' and 'Last of England' series, the 'Caravaggio Suite' and a series of worked photographs, 'St George and the Dragon').[3]

This interaction of fine art and film is paralleled by that between architecture and film. Jarman became interested in architecture when he was very young and it played a major part in his life.[4] Buildings are significant in several of his films: in *The Devils* for Ken Russell he set out to create a unique architectural environment for the events of the film, avoiding the hackneyed 'movie Gothic' style;[5] he selected Stoneleigh Abbey as a setting for *The Tempest* and similarly atmospheric buildings for *Edward II* and *War Requiem* and he set *The Rake's Progress* in a series of architecturally interesting locations ranging from Piccadilly Circus to the Angel tube station.

Certain cross-disciplinary elements in his work recur throughout his career. Some are technical, such as the use of collage and objets trouvés in painting and sculpture, superimposition and complex editing in film, and combinations of prose, poetry, journal entries and philosophical musings in literary works;

15

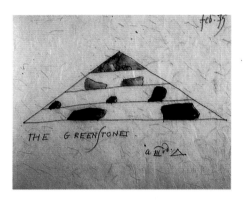

some are influences: Egypt, alchemy and Elizabethan, Jacobean and metaphysical poetry and drama; some are subjects: homosexuality, artistic creativity, the conserving and conservation of 'Englishness'; and others are types or categories of work: landscapes, figure studies or portraits – including self-portraits.

An interest in landscape is pre-eminent in Jarman's life and work. His early paintings included traditional landscapes (as well as townscapes) alongside still life, flower paintings and genre scenes. At the Slade School of Art he developed a non-figurative, spare, linear, abstracted, almost schematic style for representing what are usually flat, featureless places – beaches, seashores, deserts, plains – with distant natural features: mountain ranges, sand bars, pyramids, upright posts and indeterminate monuments (pp. 56–9).

These were exhibited widely in the late 1960s (Lisson Gallery; *Young Contemporaries at the Tate*; *Edinburgh Open 100*; *The English Landscape Tradition in the Twentieth Century* at the Camden Arts Centre; and *Drawing* at the Museum of Modern Art, Oxford). The landscapes culminated in the late 1970s in a series which were etched on slate. Towards the end of his life, he returned to the subject with many small Dungeness landscapes using a thick impasto and a range of bright, primary colours. The change from the monochrome early landscapes using thinly applied paint to the thick, multicolour late landscapes (pp. 124–5) is partly due to Jarman's use of pitch in the late 1980s, when he set objets trouvés and a variety of bric-à-brac in a tarred surface, and partly to the deterioration in his eyesight caused by AIDS and its complications.

Above: 'The Green Stones' for 'Corfe Castle film', February 1975, from Film Projects Notebook A1, Sloane Square 1975
Below: First Slade etching (untitled), 1966

OPPOSITE
Untitled drawing, charcoal, 1962?

Genius loci

Apart from a few early works, none of Jarman's paintings is in any sense naturalistic. They do not set out to capture a particular view of the countryside but rather encapsulate and explore the nature and experience of a particular place. There is often, in the 1960s work, a dreamlike, surreal aspect, which is also explored in many of the films (for example, in *The Art of Mirrors*, *Sebastiane*, *The Garden* and *Blue*) – not a familiar geographical landscape but an eternal celestial one – as well as in some of the music videos.[6]

This 'sense of place' is also found towards the end of Jarman's life in his paintings entitled or inscribed *Ego et in Arcadia* (p. 157) and *The fifth quarter of the globe*.[7] These paintings are not landscapes but do, nonetheless, convey 'a sense of place', as do his use of his parents' home movies, his own garden and Dungeness in several of his feature films (for example, *The Garden* and *The Last of England*). The use of home movies in the films recalls a sense of security in an England and an order of society that is past (*The Last of England*, *The Garden* and *Jubilee*) or creates a feeling of familiarity amidst alienation (*The Garden*).

On gardens and gardening

One special form of landscape with which Jarman was much concerned was the garden. His interest in gardening was established and encouraged early. His father's postings with the RAF meant that he grew up amidst some beautiful gardens[8] and this early interest was cemented when at the age of four he was given a book about flowers and how to grow them. At his prep school he won prizes for gardening (and when he left Hordle House he gave the school a hundred rose bushes for its walled garden). Although Canford School did not provide much scope for gardening (though it is set in parkland) there was a garden at home in Northwood.

Jarman's first forays into garden design were for fictional gardens (for *Don Giovanni* and *The Devils*). Both were formal gardens with obelisks, pyramids, topiary and hedge-lined alleys (pp. 60, 90). In 1973 there was an opportunity to create a garden for his sister and her husband at The Verzons near Ledbury, Herefordshire. It was to follow the pattern set in the two fictional gardens, with topiary, manicured hedges and obelisks. Jarman's preparatory drawings (p. 60) include an abstract garden with irregularly shaped features, a 'special garden', a series of small individual gardens, like theatre boxes, a geometrically planted orchard and several garden buildings, including a temple. There was also to be a planted maze and garden sculpture – 'antique' busts made by Jarman's long-time collaborator, Christopher Hobbs. The result would have been in the 16th- to 17th-century Franco-Italian tradition. Unfortunately nothing remains at the site.

Looking at the designs for these formal gardens might suggest that Jarman's landscapes can be seen as gardens writ large – pyramids, obelisks and foothills functioning as vista-closures or viewing points. Even the occasional monolith can be read within a garden tradition, particularly an oriental tradition; this relationship is found in Jarman's major garden achievement at Dungeness, which has much in common with the Japanese 'level garden' (hira-nimwa) and the 'literary garden' (bunjin-zukuri) with their use of sand, stone and upright features (stone in Japan, wood and metal in Jarman's case; pp. 153–6).[9]

Egypt

Despite visits to Greece and Italy, the mainstream classical world of Greece and Rome was not a major influence on Jarman's work (although we should note the series of paintings of statues and architectural fragments – p. 54). There is, however, evidence of a strong interest in Egyptian culture and history. As a child he passed through the Suez Canal en route to and from Karachi, a fleeting visit which may have influenced him (is that where the many desert landscapes derive from?). No doubt his education would have included

Jarman in his hammock with two capes displayed on the wall of his Bankside studio, 1971

Study for *Poussin's Inspiration of the Poet*, 1965

something of Egyptian history, and his interest was fed by long discussions when he was at King's College with a friend who had lived in Egypt.[10] It is present in the early landscapes with their pyramids and deserts; it recurs in his 8 mm films of the 1970s (*The Art of Mirrors*, *In the Shadow of the Sun* and *A Garden at Luxor*, pp. 8–9)[11] and the minuscule kneeling figures which populate some of his later landscapes are surely derived from Egyptian wall paintings, sculpture and hieroglyphics.[12]

Jarman's interest in alchemy also provides an Egyptian connection, albeit a tenuous one. His interest, it must be stressed, was historical and scholarly, not practical. He had no belief in magic practices or the ideas of practitioners such as Alisteir Crowley.[13] What interested him was the way the hermetic, religious writings attributed to Hermes Trismegistus (who was taken to be an Egyptian priest) were rediscovered and re-interpreted during the Renaissance and developed by pioneer chemists, mathematicians and astronomers such as

Giordano Bruno, Henry Cornelius Agrippa, the Elizabethan magus John Dee, Robert Fludd, Isaac Newton and Johannes Kepler.[14] In turn these interests were complemented by his interest in the early Greek philosopher Heraclitus both interests combined to produce iconography, symbolism, titles, characters and subject matter to many paintings in the 1980s, films including *Jubilee* and *The Tempest*, several of the music videos and his book on colour, *Chroma*. Since fire and water are key aspects of alchemical experiments and the Heraclitean idea of cyclical regeneration, and gold was the object of much alchemical work, it is not difficult to account for the regular appearance of fire in Jarman's work, the increasing use of gold with black and then red (with echoes of fire) in the 1980s paintings and the regular occurrence of expanses of water in some of the early paintings, the feature films (*Sebastiane*, *The Garden* and *The Tempest*) and several of the music videos.[15] Some paintings have titles taken from the Heraclitus fragments, such as 'The name of the bow is life its work is death' (fragment LXXIX) and 'Death is all things we see awake, all we see asleep is sleep' (fragment LXXXIX), while 'Render unto Caesar' has a card attached to the back stating 'Seekers of gold dig up much earth and find little' (fragment VIII).[16]

Artistic influences

At school Jarman studied the Impressionists and Post-Impressionists, in particular Van Gogh and Gauguin, and, perhaps later, Monet. He painted *Monet in his Garden* while he was at the Slade, and visited the garden at Giverny. A film project on Monet never came to fruition. When he was in London, Paul Nash, de Chirico,[17] Giacometti, Kitaj and even Magritte were influential figures, together with Poussin (Jarman's version of *Inspiration of the Poet* was also painted when he was at the Slade; see also p. 55).

Paul Nash's *The Pyramids in the Sea* (1912), *The Equivalents for the Megaliths* (1935) and *Landscape of the Megaliths* (1937)[18] de Chirico's deserted piazzas and townscape and paintings such as Magritte's 1932 *Mental Calculus* are examples of works that have a clear relationship to Jarman's 1960s

Jarman with *Poussin's Inspiration of the Poet*, c. 1965

landscapes. Nash's life was similar to Jarman's in several ways – his love of the Wiltshire–Dorset area; his home on the Kent coast, his premature death, his concern for landscape, megaliths, history and archaeology, his interest in surrealism and the combination of painting with, in Nash's case, photography and, in Jarman's, film.

When Jarman was at King's College, his painting *We Wait and Wait* (p. 51) was submitted to the University of London Union and *Daily Express* Art Exhibition in May 1961, and was joint winner of the amateur category, while Hockney won the professional category.[19] Hockney achieved immediate success after art school and received a commission from the *Sunday Times* in 1963 to visit Egypt (Cairo, Alexandria and Luxor) to produce drawings for their new Magazine section.[20] There is a similarity between the Jarman landscapes with pyramids and Hockney's 1963 *Sphinx and Pyramid* and *The Sphinx* and between the mask that Jarman used in *The Art of Mirrors* and *The Shadow of the Sun* and the 'object' in Hockney's 1963 *Object in the Cairo Museum*.[21]

Hockney and Jarman both achieved success in theatre design early in their careers and returned to it with great success. Hockney had not studied theatre design at the RCA, but nonetheless was invited to design *Ubu Roi* for the Royal

Paul Nash, *The Equivalents for the Megaliths*, oil, 1935

Court Theatre in London in 1966; and Jarman designed *Jazz Calendar* for the Royal Ballet in 1968. Hockney's success with his figurative painting and linear style is perhaps one of the principal reasons for Jarman's decision to adopt a different approach, forging his own way with different subject matter and style.

Abstraction and Figuration

Jarman produced few works in the 1960s and 1970s which were more abstracted than his mostly white, green or yellow landscapes. He had painted portraits, self-portraits and figure studies of various sorts up until his time at the Slade when he tended to eschew the human and animal form, apart from the minuscule ant-like figures found in some of the landscapes. He did produce a few variants on geometric and colour-field painting (on a small scale) while at the Slade or soon after, paintings such as *Recession*, the orange untitled work from 1969, the *Drawing for the First Happening*, *Construction* and *Long Graves* which were both exhibited at the Lisson Gallery (pp. 52–3).

Jarman produced a series of capes in the 1970s. The first were made of transparent plastic to which were attached flotsam and jetsam from the Thames or dollar bills (p. 12), or were decorated with alchemical symbols. Later capes

Archeologies, 1977, engraved slate

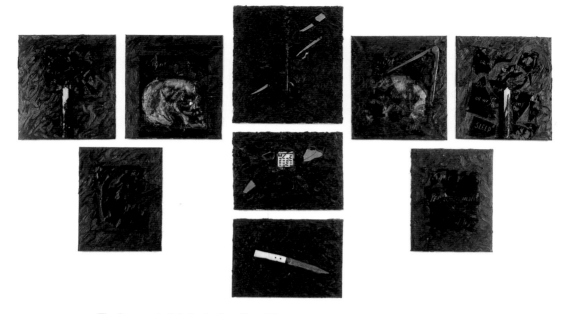

'The Caravaggio Suite', mixed media, 1986

were made of opaque materials, many coloured blue (p. 61). Apart from these it was not until the 1980s that he started to produce works that might be called 'abstract', using alchemical and Heraclitean ideas for their titles and iconography (*Mercurius*, *Soul Boy* and *Night Life*). Most of the large late paintings are abstracts. While they are very precise in the message they convey through the integrated use of text and photocopies of tabloid newspapers, they are not figurative.

The black and gold paintings

During the late 1970s Jarman produced fewer paintings. It was his stage design work for Ken Russell at the Pergola Theatre in Florence, where he designed a production of Stravinsky's *The Rake's Progress* (1982), that sent him back to painting in a new style, with new materials and renewed vigour. His set designs included, for the bordello scene, giant Michelangelesque ignudi figures over-powering the characters on stage (p. 28). The same idea was used in the Mantis Dance Company production *Mouth of the Night* in 1985 with a similar giant falling figure on one side of the stage and a large skull on the other (p. 94), and culminated in the mid-1980s with his series of six very large, unstretched and unframed canvases, 'The Last of England', which encapsulated his vision of a Britain engulfed by the forces of repression and disintegration following the coming to power of Margaret Thatcher.[22] Jarman brought back some gold leaf left over from the 1982 production and used it in some new paintings. Apparently he first covered a canvas with it, then applied black paint and scratched a design through. One example is an untitled painting of statue fragments (1982); another much later is *Fuck Me Blind* (1993) where the text is scratched through black to an eau de nil base colour (p. 131). More black and gold paintings followed (with gold paint and Dutch gold replacing gold leaf); many, but not all, were figurative: *The name of the bow is life its work is death*; the 'Perfect Strangers' series and some of the series 'Night Life'; and the self-portrait, *Old Mortality*.

Apart from Michelangelo, other influences on this phase of Jarman's work can be identified – for example El Greco and Caravaggio, Ad Reinhardt and Yves Klein. The influence of the first two is spiritual and inspirational rather than literal. With the last two Jarman was influenced, to varying extents, by their monochrome paintings, and in Klein's case by his performance work, his unconventional approach and general attitude.

Standing against Pop

When Jarman completed his Slade course the fashionable style was Pop art and the fashionable place was the USA. Jarman stood out against both (although he did visit the USA and Canada several times in the late 1960s and 1970s) but he did embrace another significant movement, that of performance art, or as it was more popularly known at that time, 'happenings'. His

Above: *The Inheritance*, mixed media, 6 November 1986
Below: *The Instruments of Her Passion*, mixed media, August 1987

interest in this area derived, on the one hand, from his theatre design experience and, on the other, from his awareness of avant garde activity. Towards the end of his time at the Slade and later he often took part in performances and happenings involving his circle of friends and collaborators, including Andrew and Peter Logan, Michael and Robbie Ginsberg, Gerald Incandela, Luciana Martinez and Christopher Hobbs. There are several untitled and unidentified drawings, for costumes or sets.[23] These performances were also the subject of several of his early Super 8 films and they are documented by photographs.

Assemblage and text

The black and gold paintings in turn gave way to assemblages in some of which he placed found and acquired objects on a base layer of pitch or oils (pp. 121–3). In other works he returned to introducing text, but on a larger scale than before. In some works he combined the two. In both cases he was able by the use of these additional elements to convey a more direct and stronger social, political, cultural or sexual message, usually with great wit and humour.

The principal influences here were Kurt Schwitters, Joseph Cornell, Robert Rauschenberg (an artist who had influenced his *Orpheus* designs while he was at the Slade) and Cy Twombly. The first three artists all contributed something to his use of assemblage and collage, especially three-dimensional collage in the case of Cornell and Schwitters, and the use of text as an integral part of the work in the case of Schwitters, Rauschenberg and Twombly.

These works repay consideration in the light of Jarman's interest in film superimposition; montages of positive and negative, black and white, colour, tinted and untinted sequences in his films and videos; and in the books, the interweaving of journal entries, autobiography, personal philosophizing, gardening notes, social and political campaigning, poetry and commonplace book composition.

Jarman often wrote the titles on works: for example in *Bound Together for Eternity*, *What if the present were the world's last night*, *Which Heaven did these keys unlock*, *Death is all things we see awake. All we see asleep is sleep* (in Greek) and *How many people has the Holy Bible killed?* On other works there are more extended texts: 'Dear God please send me to hell, Yours Derek Jarman. Dear God, If you insist on reincarnation please promise me that I will be queer though I've heard you don't approve. I'll go down on my knees. Yours faithfully Derek Jarman. Dear God You really are being most difficult. If you really are in charge surely you could grant these simple and heartfelt requests. If not make mine OBLIVION Yours in anticipation Derek Jarman'; and the following, from *Letter to the Minister* (p. 126):

Copies Sent to the Arts Minister
Dear William Shakespeare
I am a 14 year old and I'm
Queer like you I'm learning
Art I wanted to be a queer artist
Like Leonardo or Michelangelo
But I like Francis Bacon best
I read Allen Ginsberg Rimbaud
I love Tchaikovsky If I make films
I will make them like Eisenstein Murnau
Pasolini Visconti love from Derek.

These statements present explicit social and political messages. In some of his feature films, *Jubilee*, *The Last of England*, *War Requiem* and even in some of the music videos (eg, for Easterhouse and the Smiths), Jarman commented on the breakdown in British society under the Thatcher governments; on the hypocrisy of patriotism; and in *Sebastiane*, *Edward II* and, to some extent, in *Caravaggio* and *The Garden*, on society's and the church's opposition to homosexuality. In his paintings he used ironic and cutting juxtapositions of objects, as in *Crucifixion*, *In Memoriam*, *The Mistake* and *Untitled (Christ)*, and witty but pointed texts such as 'Dear God please send me to hell, Yours Derek Jarman'.

Many of the late paintings are painted over photocopied pages from the homophobic tabloid press: Jarman would then add a title written into the paint across the surface of the work. Several 'Queer' paintings have titles directly related to the tabloids and their homophobia while some of the 'Evil Queen' paintings have titles chosen by Jarman to suit his mood at the time.[24]

Other titles are concerned with HIV and AIDS. Some dealt with Jarman's own health: *TB or not TB*, *The Question*, *Sightless*, *CMV*, *Virus* and *Untitled (one day's pills)*[25]. Others drew on public perception of the illness and the tabloid press's reporting of it: *Germs* and *Infection*, the triptych *Love*, *Sex* and *Death*, *Spread the Plague*, *Arse-Injected Death Syndrome* and *Blood* all underline the role the press played in conveying alarmist misinformation and isolating the gay community.

Studio production

The later 'Queer' and 'Evil Queen' paintings have been criticized because Jarman, being too ill to work single-handed, employed assistants.[26] At least as far back as his Slade days, he always combined work undertaken individually with work produced by collaborative effort. He remarked that he preferred the theatre room at the Slade to the painting room because 'I like working on shared projects.... There is much greater aesthetic freedom... I can employ

Above: The Bordello in *The Rake's Progress* in Florence, 1982
Below: David Hockney's set for the Bordello in *The Rake's Progress*, Glyndebourne Festival Opera, 1975

imagery I would not dare or wish to use in my painting'.[27] As a film-maker Jarman was always working in a collaborative enterprise, although as director he was in ultimate control. Theatre design always has a strong collaborative basis because so many people's wishes have to be taken into account.

Some productions call for detailed drawings by the designer from which the set-builders and wardrobe department or costumiers work; others, particularly with small scale and experimental theatre and dance groups, may be created by team effort under the guidance and control of the designer. For the 1985 Mantis Dance Company production *Mouth of the Night* no drawings were produced and the design decisions and set production emerged from group discussions; yet there can be no doubt that this was a Jarman design. One only has to compare it with the designs for *The Rake's Progress* three years earlier, which were produced much more formally for Ken Russell in Florence, for which there are notebooks full of sketches and finished design drawings to see this.

For his last theatre designs, Jarman was too ill or too busy to undertake commissions single-handed. In 1991, he designed sets for *Waiting for Godot* jointly with Madeleine Morris.[28] They wanted non-naturalistic designs, but the main actors (Rik Mayall and Adrian Edmondson), the director (Les Blair) and the producer (Phil McIntyre) all wanted a naturalistic set. The result was a compromise in which Morris worked up ideas that she and Jarman developed after design conferences with the others: an abstracted landscape derived from the south-east Essex marshes with a wind-bent pollarded willow. In his final stage show, *The Maids*, Jarman worked with Nicole Robinson.[29] The relatively simple set and costumes were produced at meetings over breakfast at Maison Bertaux (a café in Soho) and on the set. All agreed that it should be simple and uncluttered (a bed and a dressing table) and Robinson kept everything suitably filthy by emptying the previous night's Hoover-bags over the set every day.[30]

Jarman was thus used to working as director of a team of professionals in realizing his designs and creative ideas in theatre and film, and it would be perfectly natural for him to extend the same methods, when ill health or pressure of work required, into the painter's studio. Most of the last paintings were indeed produced with assistants but the key artistic decisions, such as paint-mixing and application, remained firmly under his control. To suggest that the late paintings are in some way devalued because they do not carry the personal imprint of the artist's hand is to miss the point of the works, to be ignorant of Jarman's method and to ignore the studio practice that has dominated the world's great artistic cultures.

At the beginning of this essay I suggested that Jarman's success in a range of media was due to his pursuit of his interests in any media available to him, and the fact that he was his own man. His use of so many media was informed by a unified and coherent objective in each case: to explore and present his ideas in the most effective way open to him. He was clearly no mere follower of artistic fashion. He stated his belief as a film director that he should only make films that were derived from his own personal experiences and thoughts. This made it extremely difficult to raise money; his work did not interest the usual commercial sources of funding. As a painter, he did not aim to satisfy the market and the Bond Street apparatus, but rather pursued his own agenda without regard for the saleability of his work. As a gay man he chose to take a highly visible public stance on gay rights and AIDS rather than, as he might have done, maintain a reticent silence on his own sexuality. Whether painting, designing, writing about his life, designing, or making films and music videos, his work carries a personal imprint. Like one of his heroes, William Blake, Derek Jarman was always his own man – as an artist and as an individual.

1   I distinguish between his feature films intended for general release and made in 16 mm or 35 mm, and his 'artist's' films, made in Super 8 or on video, for showing to friends, or in galleries. The music videos are very much like Jarman's other films and paintings in their iconography, influences, technical construction and characteristics. They deserve further consideration (see *Sound and Vision: The Music Video Reader*, ed. Frith, Goodwin and Grossberg, Routledge, London 1993).

2   For example, *The Garden* and *War Requiem. The Last of England* is named after a Ford Madox Brown painting; *Savage Messiah*, about the sculptor Henri Gaudier-Brzeska, includes reconstructed artworks. The set for *The Rake's Progress* includes paintings by Hockney, Hogarth and Reynolds.

3   These worked photographs are variously dated 1979 and 1981. The image is taken from the film *Arty the Pose* and was re-used in *The Dream Machine*.

4   Robin Noscoe, the art master at Canford School, designed his own house. Jarman was among those who helped build it. At King's he was taught by Nikolaus Pevsner and went on field trips with him. Jarman later appeared in one of the BBC 'Building Sights' series about the Noscoe house; and he played a large part in a 1984 project in which the avant-garde architecture group NATO, led by Nigel Coates, designed a house for him. Carlos Villanueva Brandt, a member of the group, remembers that Jarman 'was a brilliant "architect"'. He had spatial awareness and recognized the difference between direct and reflected and diffused light'. Coates recalled that Jarman talked about 'what he wanted and how he would live in it…. He was very specific about the site.'

5   'My architectural style is movie gothick southern style…it makes no attempt at the nasty Banister Fletcher realism of most commercial movie sets' (undated letter from Jarman to Dom Sylvester Houedard in the Houedard papers, Derek Jarman letters file no. 2. With acknowledgments to the John Rylands University Library of Manchester).

6   For example 'Panic' by the Smiths, '1969' by Easterhouse, 'It's a Sin' by the Pet Shop Boys and 'In the Pouring Rain' by Bob Geldof.

7   This title is derived from a Roman name for the Dungeness area.

8   Among them the Villa Zuassa on Lake Maggiore; in Rome, their flat on the Via Paisiello was close to the Villa Borghese gardens; and their rented manor house at Curry Mallet in Somerset.

9   It is interesting to look at Dungeness alongside gardens in Japan such as the Ryuan-Ji and

Myoshin-Ji temple and the Sento Gosho and Tofukuji gardens at Kyoto.

10 Pat, later wife of Lawrence Warwick-Evans, who shared a flat with Jarman in the 1960s.

11 Also *Akhenaten*, an unrealized film project for which jewel-like drawings exist.

12 For example, *The Book of the Dead* (British Museum Press, London 1993, pp. 14, 24–5, 45, 106–7) and statues of a priest holding an offering table and of Iti (British Museum nos. 21979 and 24429).

13 In *Chroma*, Jarman says that he 'stumbled into alchemy reading Jung's *Alchemical Studies* early in the 1970s' (p. 75). His interest was wider than simply studying its history. He drew a parallel between the alchemist's activity and that of a film-maker: 'Film is the wedding of light and matter – an alchemical conjunction'.

14 He was familiar with work on this subject by the historian Frances Yates, also her books on the Elizabethan stage, the art of memory, the Elizabethan cult of Astraea and Shakespeare's last plays.

15 Paintings include *Philosopher's Egg, Mercurius, Fool's Gold* and *The Gold Stone*; videos include Marianne Faithfull ('Broken English' – note the use of gold for the mask), the Smiths ('The Queen is Dead'), the Pet Shop Boys ('It's a Sin'), Billy Hyena ('Wide Boy Awake'), Suede ('The Next Life'), Marc Almond ('Tenderness is a Weakness') and Bob Geldof ('I cry too').

16 The fragments are numbered according to *The Art and Thought of Heraclitus*, ed. Charles H. Kahn, Cambridge University Press 1979. In fragment LXXIX it is impossible to distinguish the archaic Greek words in written form for 'life' and 'bow'. Fragment LXXXIX goes to the heart of Heraclitus's theories of life and death and cyclical regeneration.

17 Jarman said he silently dedicated his first major exhibition to de Chirico (*Dancing Ledge*, p. 82).

18 Nash's influence is most obviously seen in Jarman's Avebury paintings. I must thank Charlotte and William Ford for alerting me to these particular works.

19 Jarman's co-winner was David Kunzle from the Courtauld Institute. The prize was £20.

20 In fact the work was not published in the magazine.

21 Collection Galerie Claude Bernard, Paris, private collection and Collection Paul Kasmin, New York respectively. All were exhibited in *David Hockney: A Drawing Retrospective* in London 1995.

22 In the series a map of England, Scotland and Wales is engulfed by fire, smoke and flame.

23 For example, *Drawing for the First Happening, The Tree a wire pagoda* and *Set for yellow and blue dancers*.

24 Jarman engaged with a range of issues arising from his homosexuality in his work from the 1970s onwards, in film, painting and in his writing; it was in no way a subject that he came to only in the late work. Questions of gay rights and the marginalization of gays are germane to his 'political' films (such as *Jubilee* and *The Last of England*) as well as the overtly homoerotic and gay films (such as *Sebastiane, The Garden, Edward II, Wittgenstein, Caravaggio* and *Blue*). *The Garden* and *Caravaggio* are the most significant of the films in which he engaged with the Christian church(es) over their attitude to homosexuality – a subject that also frequently occurs in the late assemblages.

25 The first incorporates drip bags and an oxygen mask, the last one day's supply of medication. *Sightless* uses photographs of Jarman's eyes and *The Question* uses X-rays.

26 Piers Clemmet and later Karl Lydon.

27 *Dancing Ledge* p. 74.

28 Madeleine Morris has designed for Operating Theatre Company, Company of Clerks, Cherub, the Claire Russ Ensemble, Eddie Izzard, Sylvie Guillem (for the BBC) and films funded by the BFI and Channel 4. She won London New Play Festival Best Designer award in 1993.

29 Nicole Robinson is a performance artist and dancer who had studied at Wimbledon College of Art (performance, film and dance). Since graduating she has danced professionally, worked for a theatrical costumier and made costumes for her own performance works.

30 Actresses Tania and Michele Wade and Chris Peyton, the director, contributed to the decisions.

An Archaeology of Soul

Gray Watson, course leader, MA Critical Studies in Visual Art and Theatre,
Wimbledon School of Art

Probably the two qualities which struck almost everyone who met Derek Jarman
most forcibly were his energy and his generosity of spirit. To these should
be added his humour, his honesty and, especially towards the end of his life,
his truly heroic courage. He also undoubtedly had, as not many artists do,
a genuinely individual vision.

His energy was legendary, and for many it was a powerful source of
inspiration. As Colin McCabe wrote in his excellent obituary of Jarman in the
Independent, 'to encounter the man himself in the streets of Soho and to discuss
with manic intensity a dozen projects in fewer minutes was to be re-energised
and revitalised for weeks.'[1] Even knowing Jarman's level of energy, however, it
was still almost impossible to believe that, since being diagnosed HIV positive
at the end of 1986, he could have managed in the seven years remaining to him
to direct six more feature films, write five more books (not counting extended
film scripts), paint as many pictures as some painters would in an entire lifetime,
and create a garden whose originality has earned it a place in gardening history,
as well as campaigning tirelessly for queer (the word he came to prefer) causes –
all this while much of the time suffering from the most appalling symptoms,
including, in the later stages of his illness, motor dysfunction and blindness.

This extraordinary achievement was helped by the fact that Jarman had
never been a perfectionist. As he said to Lynn Barber, 'I don't suffer from
perfectionism. The thing is you mustn't be precious about things, and then
you can get a lot done.'[2] This lack of perfectionism was linked to a certain
impatience, a quality of which he was aware from early on. Referring to his
painting activity during the late 1960s, he wrote: 'I was impatient, wanted quick
immaculate results, hated "the struggle".'[3] The negative side of this was, it must
be admitted, an occasional unevenness of artistic quality, at the worst making
for quite slipshod results. The positive side, however, was an extraordinary
freedom from inhibiting blockages: from the thinking of a thought to the
carrying out of the corresponding action the passage was direct and immediate.
This both prevented creative energy from being squandered, and facilitated the
free flow of ideas and images from the unconscious.

Jarman's openness to the unconscious was linked to an openness to chance
effects, an ability to make creative use of accident. This partly accounts for

his tendency to take whatever happened to be going on in his life at any given moment and transform it into a theme of universal, almost mythic, significance. That tendency also reflected, however, Jarman's immensely strong sense of ego, another reason no doubt for his prodigious accomplishment. A close friend and colleague has likened him to 'an egomaniacal jellyfish floating on the warm currents of the world's oceans'. If he was constantly absorbing inspiration from everything and everyone around him, his personal vision was so powerful that whatever he absorbed tended to be subsumed into that vision rather than ever being allowed to deflect him from it.

Between worlds, between media

Jarman's activity was characterized at the same time by the breadth of its scope and the unity of its purpose. There was no hard-and-fast distinction between his personal life, his homosexual campaigning and his art, nor between the different artistic media and contexts in which he worked. He moved freely between several visual media, and between the visual in general and the verbal, often creating interesting new permutations; in the same way he moved freely, and in the process helped forge new links, between the art world, the film world, the theatre world and the gay world.

His approach was inclusive, not exclusive; never a dogmatist or purist, he tended towards multi-dimensionality and multi-textuality, as his liking for such devices as palimpsest, layering and superimposition suggests. There is something richly theatrical about his work, and although he did once say, in relation to his paintings at the end of the 1980s, that 'theatrical acts are for the theatre, not for painting',[4] theatricality is in fact as present in his paintings as it is in his films.

Equally, however, there is a sense in which Jarman was always essentially a painter. This is certainly how he came increasingly to describe himself towards the end of his life. A good case could be made for the view that his sensibility as a painter was also the principal factor behind his originality as a film-maker. As he himself said in relation to his films, 'I've always taken a great interest in form. It's part of a painter's training, form and content.' Mark Nash, in his article 'Innocence and Experience', noted the relevance to the films of both visual art and theatre design: 'Jarman's films work outwards from tableaux, recalling painting or sculpture…. Staging, art direction, image are the most important qualities…. Narrative takes second place.'[5]

Jarman began his career as a painter and the very last works that he made, just before his death, were paintings: he had spoken several times, with prophetic empathy, about Matisse's last work, his *papiers découpés* (paper cut-outs), and whilst Jarman's own last paintings were utterly different from Matisse's, coming closer both stylistically and in terms of method to Abstract Expressionism, there was the same transmutation of the limited means which health permitted into an opportunity for a new and final burst of creative originality.

Doubtless it is a coincidence, but it is nevertheless striking how the development of Jarman's painting style falls neatly into decades. During the 1960s he was painting sensitive but somewhat tight landscapes which, unlike his contemporaneous theatre work, were becoming ever emptier. As he later recalled in *The Last of England*, 'their titles tell the story: *Stony Ground, Cool Waters*. My final picture of the decade was called *Deserts*. Then I picked up a Super 8 camera in 1970 and started to populate these dreary pictures with my friends.'[6]

If the 1970s were the decade in which he established himself in film, the 1980s saw him, alongside his films, making predominantly black paintings, in which his interest in alchemy became especially evident and which culminated in the exhibition *Luminous Darkness* in Tokyo in 1990. As the decade progressed, the black paint was applied in a thicker impasto, into which were embedded broken glass and a vast array of other objects from bullets to crucifixes to condoms to old photographs, some of the later works dispensing with paint altogether. These 1980s assemblages can be seen as belonging to a tradition stemming from Schwitters, Ernst and Cornell. Finally, in the 1990s, Jarman's painting style changed again, to become more definitely painterly, using a full range of colours, and culminating in the series of violently expressive pictures which were exhibited at the Whitworth Gallery, Manchester, shortly after his death. In these, as Ken Butler describes, 'handfuls of paint were scooped from tins and literally flung on to the canvas or smeared on with both hands,'[7] in an attempt to release some of the anger he felt about having AIDS.

His picking up of a Super 8 camera in 1970 had more or less coincided with his being commissioned to design the sets for Ken Russell's *The Devils*. His work with Russell then and subsequently on *Savage Messiah* introduced him to the world of relatively mainstream cinema; and there is no doubt that this experience played an important formative part in his own career as a director. However, it was his experiments with Super 8 that led him to create a type of cinema that was uniquely his own.

Jarman's films need to be seen first of all within a tradition of artistic avant-garde film-making, and in particular that tradition of American avant-garde film whose leading figure was Stan Brakhage, and which was superbly chronicled by P. Adams Sitney in his *Visionary Film*, a book that Jarman respected enormously. Most films in that tradition were made in 16 mm, rather than the 35 mm of commercial cinema; the still smaller Super 8 was much more rare, although Brakhage himself did use it for an important series of films. It was Jarman,

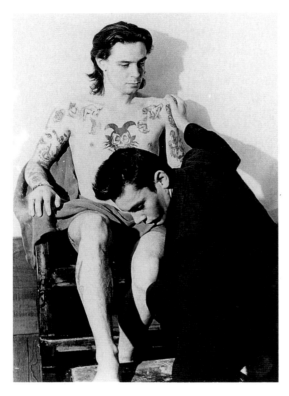

Dave Baby, Philip Williamson, *The Angelic Conversation*, 1985

however, who made this gauge peculiarly his own, exploiting its possibilities to the full. The breakthrough came in 1973 with *The Art of Mirrors*, of which he wrote in his diary: 'this is something which could only be done on a Super 8 camera, with its built-in meters and effects. At last we have something completely new.'[8] It was also important because, even more than 16 mm, it gave financial independence. As Jarman said, 'the Super 8 camera is free. 35 mm is chained by money to the institutions… economics have gutted mind from the format.' One is reminded of Cocteau's remark that film will never become an art form until its materials are as cheap as pencil and paper.

The home movie connotations of Super 8 (largely inherited by video), which might be an embarrassment for some, Jarman turned to positive advantage. At times he almost seemed to be suggesting some filmic archetype: 'The home movie is bedrock…. In all home movies is a longing for paradise.'[9] His own 'home movies' were of course unusual in that they did not depict conventional family life, but there was considerable poignancy, for example, in his incorporation of some of his father's home-movie footage, of himself and his mother when he was a child, into *The Last of England*. He was also alluding to the significance of home-movie making, in the more traditional family sense, in a sequence with Prospero and Miranda in *The Tempest*. As Gaia Shaw says:

Prospero's potency is symbolised in his magic staff. It is shaped in the zodiac symbol for Mercury…and at the top is a magic mirror of memory. Through this Prospero shows his daughter Miranda an image of herself as a child…. Here we are being shown the magical quality of the home-movie: to allow a father to share a visual experience of memory with his child.[10]

It should be noted that Jarman cast his own niece as the infant Miranda and that the whole film was dedicated to the memory of his mother.

While Jarman was especially creative with the hand-held Super 8 and video camera, he was equally creative when transferring footage from one medium to another. As well as just blowing up from Super 8 to 35 mm, he would transfer material from film to video, and from video to film, employing a wide range of techniques, including the refilming of images projected onto a screen, as was the case, for example, with *The Angelic Conversation*. It is in films such as these, which make most use of the formal properties of film and/or video – the ones, that is, which could most easily be described as 'painterly' or 'poetic' – that Jarman made the greatest aesthetic innovations and in which, in a sense, he was most completely in control. The closer he approached normal commercial cinema, the more uncertain his grasp became.

Partly this reflected Jarman's difficulty in creating convincing narratives – narrative dialogue in particular – a problem which he sometimes solved by taking a readymade script, as with *The Tempest* and *Edward II*. His difficulty with narrative reflected his lack of affinity for linear thinking in general, and his preference for more loosely associative and poetic patterns of thought. This was just as evident in his books as in his films. As he wrote at the beginning of *Modern Nature*: 'my book is a series of introductions to matters and agendas unfinished. Like memory, it has gaps, amnesia, fragments of past, fractured present.'

Sex, politics and revolution

One of Jarman's motives for turning to film in 1970 had been, as he acknowledged, a fear that if he were to bring his gay life into his paintings he would be perceived as a mere follower of David Hockney. At the same time, he also recognized the stronger communicative power of film, and at least sometimes believed in its greater relevance altogether. As he wrote in *Dancing Ledge*, 'had Caravaggio been reincarnated in this century it would have been as a film-maker, Pasolini.'[11] Despite his difficulties with narrative, he ventured into a type of film-making which, if not exactly mainstream, was at least recognizable as cinema by a wider audience. One of the main reasons for this was his burning need to communicate a social message, particularly on the subject of homosexuality. 'My films,' he said, 'are a message of solidarity to people who have been dispossessed. Because when I made *Sebastiane* there was no way of imaging yourself as a gay, you wouldn't even see gays on television, so how could you come to terms with yourself?'[12]

Just as, both in his works and by personal example, he gave support and inspiration to countless men, and some women, struggling to come to terms with queer sexuality, so when he was diagnosed HIV positive he also provided a beacon to those affected, or threatened, by AIDS. The very fact of continuing to work was important, as he knew: 'To me the one thing I could do was to carry on working, so other people in the same circumstances could see it was possible.'[13] Even though nothing could take away from the pain and horror of the physical effects of the disease, it was also important to try, by making his own experiences public, to alleviate for other sufferers the added burden of shame, fear and isolation.

At the same time, Jarman directed his message to the heterosexual majority. It is possible that the propagandistic stridency of his tone, together with occasional lapses into sentimentality and an obsessional tendency to read the homosexual issue into almost every aspect of existence, may have alienated some who were in principle well disposed to his message. On the other hand, in order to produce sufficient energy to blast through certain deep-seated and often unconscious prejudices, extremism may well at times be necessary; and what is undeniable is that the message which Jarman had to communicate about homosexuality was the fruit not only of considerable first-hand experience but also of deep and sustained reflection upon it.

But whilst Jarman could speak with authority, as well as passion, about the politics of homosexuality, his views on more general political issues of the day were, reasonably enough, neither more nor less informed than those of the average citizen. As both an artist and an activist, it is hardly surprising that he should have inclined to the left, but mainly as a matter of instinct; his brief flirtation with the Workers' Revolutionary Party (WRP), under the influence of Vanessa Redgrave, bore all the signs of well-meaning naïveté. But the way in which art can make a genuine and distinctive contribution to political understanding may not be at the literal day-to-day level but in a far more indirect and subtle sense. In particular certain artists, and Jarman among them, can – through their honesty, freedom from dogma and acuity of vision – provoke speculations about long-term political and historical processes which transcend existing political and ideological paradigms.

One instance in which Jarman reflected more consciously than usual on this very issue was the project he worked on between 1979 and 1983 for a film to have been called *Neutron*. Based on Jung's *Aeon* and the Revelation of St John the Divine, it was to have combined politics with mythology, and to have had at its centre the conflict between the priorities of the political activist and those of the artist.

Jarman's brief experience with the WRP provoked some suggestively ambivalent comments in the chapter 'On Seeing Red' in *Chroma*:

Red with anger, they proclaimed the Revolution, Red Phrygian caps thrown high. The scarlet neckerchiefs of Garibaldi.... Blood, the guillotine and old women knitting scarlet.... Red rags to John Bull.... As we march, the red-necked gentlemen of England, in hunting red, are sweating away their Saturday afternoon chasing the red fox. But our eyes are focused on Lenin's tomb. The tomb of the Revolution.[14]

In the same chapter, there is a similarly suggestive ambivalence in Jarman's treatment of the related symbolism of fire: 'The child of fire is the child of disobedience. In revolt. The Promethean child steals the matches to strike a dangerous light in the dark.'[15] This deeper, more long-term political significance of fire is superbly invoked by the intercutting between torch-bearer and rioters in *The Last of England*: one is reminded of James Baldwin's *The Fire Next Time*, as well as of William Blake's Orc.

Alchemy and magic

Fire is a central feature of Jarman's extensive use of alchemical symbolism. He wrote in *The Last of England*:

Fire runs in rivulets through my dreams, consumes everything in its path. In *In the Shadow of the Sun*, it's organised in a geometric fire-maze, the roses burn.[16] The same maze occurs

Tilda Swinton dancing next to the fire in *The Last of England*, 1987

in *Jubilee*, we are literally playing in fire. Fire informs *The Last of England*.... It flickers across *Imagining October*, sacred fires of Zoroaster. Fire destroys the old, creates a place for the new. Firefly, scintilla, spark, pyromaniac. Turner's *Burning of the Houses of Parliament*, sheets of fire reflected in the waters, rivers of fire, the burning heart of the matter.[17]

If the principal alchemical significance of fire is as an agent of purification and transformation, in a process whose culmination is signified by gold, there is a sense in which the sun, in addition to being a masculine symbol, also links fire and gold directly, by virtue of its physical and visual properties. The script for a projected film *Silence Is Golden (Nijinsky's Last Dance)* describes the dancer's body being burnt to ashes, which are themselves transformed into gold in a furnace. With the words 'Washing my hands in the sun', Nijinsky dances a fire dance, 'wreathed in flames'.[18]

Unlike Turner, Jarman does not often look, or invite us to look, directly at the sun, but his interest in solar symbolism is evident. His interest in lunar symbolism, by contrast, is far less conspicuous. There are very few occasions on which moon imagery is used directly; but another of the images, along with fire, which recur most frequently in his films is that of a young man reflecting sunlight into the camera, creating a dazzle effect. For Gaia Shaw, the image symbolizes the alchemist's, and the artist's, task of guiding spirit into matter, whilst the principle is a lunar one:

the angelic lad flashes a mirror (usually round), at the sun and deflects the beam into the camera.... The act is an image of an artist guiding spirit (light) into matter (our eyes or the art work).... As a bringer of light [the young man]...is copying the principle of the moon: his dazzle is the law of Reflections.[19]

If alchemy is an important element in Jarman's films, it is equally so in his paintings, especially in the predominantly black assemblages of the 1980s. Many of these actually contain gold paint or gold leaf, whilst many also contain glass, usually broken. A particularly pure example of a work made from gold and broken glass is *Silence*, in which the words 'silence' and 'golden' are inscribed, and which also contains the remains of a light bulb, hinting at the several connotations of illumination (p. 121). Another painting in which the sense of alchemy is especially strong is *Prospect – The Shadow takes on Substance*, whose title perfectly encapsulates the relationship of these paintings to his films, and which features a large, opaque, broken mirror in an elaborate, gilded rococo frame (p. 123). Glass has, of course, many connotations, including vision, clarity and opacity; it is also especially relevant to painting, inasmuch as paintings may be thought of as providing, in varying degrees, a window on the world and

Matthew Hawkins in the disco scene in *The Last of England*, 1987

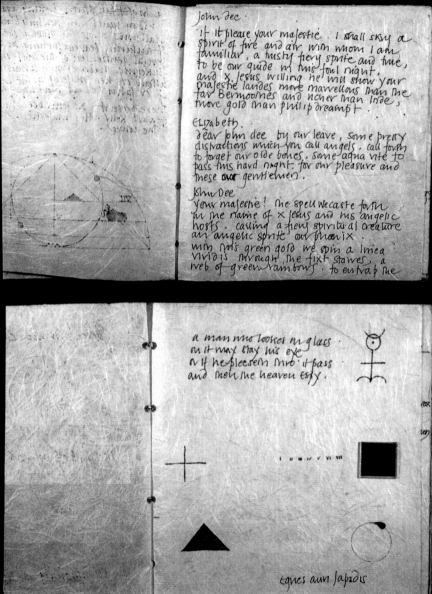

John dee.

if it please your majestie. I shall skry a
spirit of fire and air with whom I am
familiar, a lusty fiery sprite and true,
to be our guide in this foul night,
and x Jesus willing he will show your
majestie landes more marvellous than the
far Bermoothes and richer than Inde,
more gold than philip dreampt.

Elizabeth.

dear john dee by our leave, some pretty
distractions which you call angels, call forth
to forget our olde bones, some aqua vite to
pass this hard night. for our pleasure and
these our gentlemen.

John Dee.

Your majestie! the spell wecaste forth
in the name of x Jesus and his angelic
hosts. calling a fiery spiritual creature
an angelic sprite our phoenix.
with this green gold we spin a linea
viridis through the fixt starres, a
web of green rainbows. to entrap the

a man who lookes in glass.
on it may stay his eye.
or if he pleesem thro it pass
and then the heaven espy.

L U M N V VI VII

eques aum lapidis

Two pages (the one below with alchemical symbols) from a script of 'Dr Dee – The Art of Mirrors
and a Summoning of Angels', Notebook A5, October 1975

a reflection of the human soul. This partly accounts for the power of the image of broken glass in twentieth-century art, from the visual appearance of Analytical Cubist paintings through the more psychologically conscious references to it, or uses of it, by for example Duchamp, Breton and Magritte. In continuing this tradition, Jarman – for whom the act itself of breaking the glass was crucial – laid particular emphasis on the active role of the artist–magus–alchemist: initially as destroyer, finally as transformer.

Jarman read widely in the areas of psychology, magic and the occult. He suggested that Jung's *Alchemical Studies* and *Seven Sermons to the Dead* could be taken as keys to *In the Shadow of the Sun*, even though in fact he only read them after making the film. These books, he said, 'gave me the confidence to allow my dream-images to drift and collide at random'. In addition to Jung, he read James Hillman, notably such books as *Dream and the Underworld* and *Pan and the Nightmare*, and he was deeply influenced by Frances Yates's writings on the hermetic tradition in the Renaissance: Giordano Bruno and, still more, John Dee were important reference points for him, as was Henry Cornelius Agrippa's *Three Books of Occult Philosophy*, which Yates describes as 'the most important Renaissance text book on Hermetic and Cabalistic magic'.[20]

Jarman's fascination with secret societies and closed groups undoubtedly related to his experience of minority sexuality. At the same time, his interest in magic manifested itself in his attraction to hieroglyphs, symbols in which the visual and verbal are combined. The following passage is instructive, specifically in relation to his Super 8 work, but also to his work in general, since he used the hieroglyphic principle throughout:

This is the way the Super 8s are structured from writing: the buried word-signs emphasize the fact that they convey a language. There is the image and the word, and the image of the word. The 'poetry of fire' relies on a treatment of word and object as equivalent: both are luminous and opaque. The pleasure of Super 8s is the pleasure of seeing language put through the magic lantern.[21]

The Fall of Albion
The interdependence of visual and verbal elements was one of the several respects in which Jarman's work could be compared with that of William Blake. In many ways, Jarman's whole approach was very close to Blake's, and there are indeed some direct references to him, including extensive use of his poetry in *Imagining October*, and several references to his pictures in the proposed film on Nijinsky. Given, however, the extent to which Blake's eccentric, radical, anti-materialist and somewhat apocalyptic vision prefigured Jarman's own, these references are surprisingly rare.

Perhaps the feature of Blake's vision which was most crucial for Jarman, and was in fact a key to much of his work, was the personification of England as the giant Albion, the original (androgynous) Cosmic Man, an image of perfection and completeness, who is fallen (broken) and must be redeemed (re-membered). Albion, in his fallen state, was the subject of the 1984 painting series 'GBH', as well as of the films *Jubilee*, *The Last of England* and *Imagining October*. If England, this sceptred isle, has fallen into chaos and disarray, and needs to be redeemed, this is the manifestation at a national, political and historical level of an archetypal pattern of fall and redemption which embraces each individual psyche as well as the whole cosmos. It has links both with the myth of Christ, thoroughly relevant to *The Garden*, and with that of Dionysus.

Jarman's mythicization of England was rooted in a very real patriotism, almost a form of cultural High Toryism, which was unexpected in the light of some of his other attitudes. Like most of his generation, he had in 1960 been in love with everything American, but he was also, somewhat less typically, drawn to the old world: to Italy and especially to his native England, its landscape and its architecture, Ely Cathedral in particular occupying a special place in his affection. Jarman's love of English architecture had been deepened, as he often acknowledged, by his friendship with Nikolaus Pevsner; perhaps he gave less credit than he should have to the deepening of his knowledge of English literature, as well as the enriching of his whole creative vocabulary, which resulted from his time at King's College, London, before going on to be an art student at the Slade.

His love for English architecture and literature came together in *The Angelic Conversation*, based on Shakespeare's sonnets. Jarman described the film as 'a series of slow-moving sequences through a landscape seen from the windows of an Elizabethan house'. He recognized the element of nostalgia in that film, as elsewhere in his work, but was prepared to justify it: 'Elizabethan England is our cultural Arcadia, as Shakespeare is the essential pivot of our culture.'[22] He did not confuse Elizabethan England with a golden age in a straightforward historical sense, but he did believe the great Elizabethans provided a reference point to which, in our present debased age, we might usefully look back.

The great enemy, for Jarman, was the banality attendant upon commercialization:

In the short space of my lifetime I've seen the destruction of the landscape through commercialisation, a destruction so complete that fragments are preserved as if in a museum.... Canterbury is now reduced to an 'historic centre', a heritage town.... The city of pilgrims has become an empty 'theme park'. The land of England was once the

Soldiers posing for a painting in *Imagining October*, 1984

home of dryads and nymphs. Every now and then you can feel the last of them lurking around a corner: at Dancing Ledge, at Winspit.[23]

He never depicted this banality directly, except perhaps in such satirical scenes as the Judas sequence in *The Garden*. What he did show were scenes of destruction and industrial dereliction: even in *The Angelic Conversation*, the most paradisiacal of his films, there were images of burning cars and radar systems – an anarchic scene of which he ostensibly disapproved, but in which in practice he found another form of beauty.

Michael O'Pray was right to say of his depiction of social chaos in *Jubilee*: 'an energy is released which Jarman may criticize but which also enthralls him.'[24] Similarly, despite his undoubted sincerity in aligning himself with Green politics, the grim industrial wasteland of *The Last of England*, for example, was almost as Romantic a landscape as the Dorset coast. Jarman took an evident delight in the fact that his own personal paradise garden was overshadowed by the nuclear power station at Dungeness. In that sense, he went beyond Blake's disapproval of the 'dark, Satanic mills'; he came closer perhaps to the Blake of *The Marriage of Heaven and Hell*, and certainly to Baudelaire and the altogether more modern *maudit* tradition.[25] But if, as he said, he soon learned that 'decadence' was a sign of intelligence, he was certainly no flippant aesthete. On the contrary, Jarman's vision, like that of his hero Pasolini, was profoundly moral: all the more so, because of the tension resulting from his openness to the claims of evil.

Private and public worlds
Jarman's lightness and charm have sometimes obscured his seriousness of purpose, yet those very qualities, in preventing him from becoming sententious, may in part have been a token of his genuineness: one is reminded of Nietzsche's remark that he would never trust a philosopher who could not dance. For all his love of celebratory camp – evident for example in several of his early home movies and in the 'Think Pink!' section of *The Garden* – Jarman had no use at all for what he called a 'camp complicity with trash'. His fulminations against the waste of resources in mainstream, commercial cinema, that supreme purveyor of trash, were not only a complaint about financial waste but also an indictment of the squandering of cinema's ability to be the transmitter of authentic visions. But if he took no part in camp complicity, nor did he shelter, as many more intellectually pretentious visual artists do, behind postmodernist irony: endlessly quoting other people's ideas and images, whilst dressing up their inability to propose any of their own as theoretical sophistication, rather than the cowardice and lack of imagination that it is.

Probably the most important quality of art, for Jarman, was to be found in what he referred to as the 'attrition between private and public worlds'.[26] He believed the most intimate and subtle nuances of individual experience could be directly relevant to issues of the widest social significance; so that, in remaining true to these whilst endowing them with aesthetic form, the artist performed a moral and political function. That is partly why honesty was so crucial for him, and why his decision to come out publicly about being HIV positive was so typical: 'I had no choice, I've always hated secrets – the canker that destroys.'[27]

It also explains why accusations of self-indulgence were, for the most part, misconceived. All too often these accusers, whether they realized it or not, expected art to confirm some already existent ideological perspective; whereas Jarman knew that the most pertinent contribution that an artist can make is to work with those very details and nuances which cannot yet be fitted into a theoretically coherent framework – those very points at which the attrition between the private and the public is at its most uncomfortable. One of the most valuable features of Jarman's approach, which is the approach of all true artists, is that, however irritating it may be to theorists in the short run, in the long run it is what makes the refinement of understanding possible.

All Jarman's life was a process of exploration, motivated simultaneously by a desire to experience the unknown and yet paradoxically to return to some form of 'home'. In this exploration, his sexual adventures played an especially prominent part; but as an artist, he felt called upon to share his discoveries with others, and in particular with those who themselves felt drawn to a similar quest. In an extraordinary section in his book *The Last of England*, entitled 'The Sound of Breaking Glass', he came close to defining the core of his activity:

My world is in fragments, smashed in pieces so fine I doubt I will ever reassemble them. So I scrabble in the rubbish, an archaeologist who stumbles across a buried film. An archaeologist who projects his private world along a beam of light into the arena, till all goes dark at the end of the performance, and we go home. Home is where one should be… Now, I'm not going to duck it, ART is the key… it needs no money, this archaeology of soul, tho' the powers grab it and run it through the projectors to blind you. An artist is engaged in a dig. Deep down, depth, 'the way up is the way down', so it's not about bettering yourself or greening suburbia, you're more likely to meet it in the Police Constable's Cesspit.[28]

I find those who have not visited the cesspit have the stink of virtue. Now you project your private world into the public arena, and produce the flashpoint; the attrition between the private and public world is the tradition you discover. All you can do is point the direction that everyone in the audience who wishes to 'travel' has to take.[29]

1 *Independent*, 21 February 1994, p. 14.

2 *Independent on Sunday*, 4 August 1991, 'Sunday Review', pp. 2ff.

3 *Dancing Ledge*, p. 95.

4 Quoted by Elizabeth Glazebrook, *City Limits*, January 1989.

5 *Afterimage* 12, Autumn 1985, p. 32.

6 *The Last of England*, p. 54.

7 Ken Butler, 'All the Rage', in *Vogue*, December 1993, p. 158, reprinted in catalogue for exhibition *Evil Queen: The Last Paintings*, Manchester, Whitworth Art Gallery, University of Manchester, in association with Richard Salmon Ltd.

8 Quoted in *Afterimage* 12, p. 17.

9 *The Last of England*, p. 54.

10 Gaia Shaw, 'Queer Gravity: Alchemy and Sexuality in Derek Jarman's Films and Paintings', unpublished dissertation for MA in Fine Art and Theatre (Interdisciplinary Historical and Theoretical Studies), Wimbledon School of Art and University of Surrey, 1994, pp. 21–22.

11 *Dancing Ledge*, p. 9.

12 Interview with Lynn Barber, *Independent on Sunday*, 4 August 1991.

13 Interview with Mick Brown, *Daily Telegraph*, 16 August 1993.

14 *Chroma*, pp. 40–41.

15 *Ibid.*, p. 37.

16 Cf. the end of T .S. Eliot's *The Four Quartets*.

17 *The Last of England*, pp. 224–25.

18 Reproduced in *Afterimage* 12, pp. 26–29.

19 Gaia Shaw, 'Queer Gravity', p. 36.

20 Frances Yates, *The Art of Memory*, p. 206, quoted in Shaw, *op. cit.*, p. 3.

21 *Dancing Ledge*, p. 129.

22 *Afterimage* 12, p. 49.

23 *The Last of England*, pp. 136–38. Dancing Ledge and Winspit are points on the coast of the Isle of Purbeck, in Dorset.

24 Michael O'Pray, 'Derek Jarman's Cinema: Eros and Thanatos,' in *Afterimage* 12, p. 14.

25 See, for example, Georges Bataille, *Literature and Evil*. The 'poète maudit' (cursed poet) was Baudelaire's description of the poet as a victim of a cruel destiny.

26 *Dancing Ledge*, p. 236.

27 Interview with Lynn Barber, *Independent on Sunday*, 'Sunday Review' p. 5.

28 A former Chief Constable of Manchester referred to homosexuals with AIDS as 'swirling in a cesspit of their own making'.

29 *The Last of England*, pp. 235–36.

Self-Portrait, 1961?

2nd Potters Bar Fête, 1961 or before

OPPOSITE
We Wait and Wait, 1960–61
Amateur first prize (joint) in the
University of London Union/*Daily
Express* Art Exhibition 1961

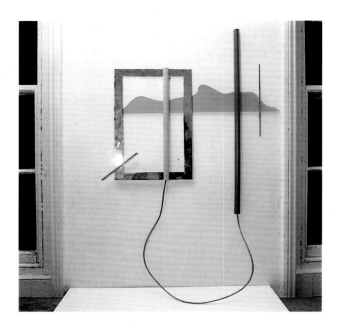

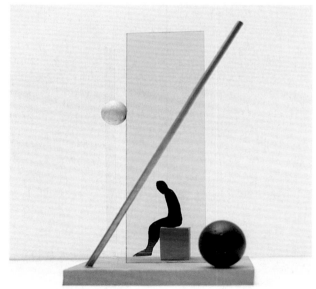

Long Graves, iron with marble grave chippings, at the Lisson Gallery, London, February–March 1969

OPPOSITE
Above: *Construction*, spring 1968
Below: Small static sculpture/figure, October 1968

Sculpture Garden, 1967

OPPOSITE
Above: *Pleasures of Italy 2*, June 1972
Below: *From Poussin's Inspiration of a Poet*, spring 1965

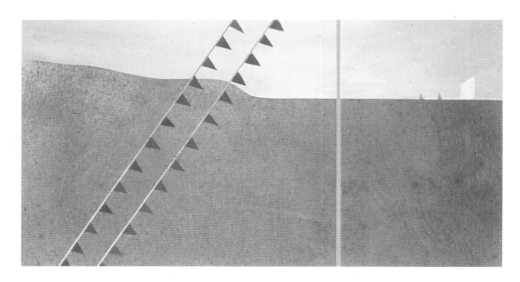

Above: Unidentified painting, possibly *The Shore*
Oil and collage on canvas, November–December 1968

Below: Untitled
Acrylic on canvas, early or mid-1970s

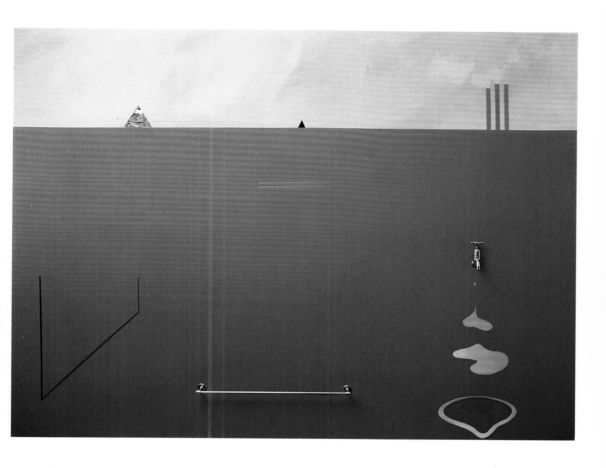

Cool Waters
Oil on canvas with tap and towel rail, 1966–67
Exhibited at *Young Contemporaries at the Tate*
(Tate Gallery) in 1967

 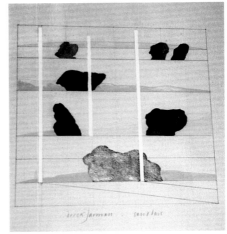

Left: Avebury Series No. 4
Oil on canvas, 1973
Right: *Sand Base*
Oil on canvas, *c.* 1973

OPPOSITE
Untitled landscape
Oil on canvas, early or mid-1970s

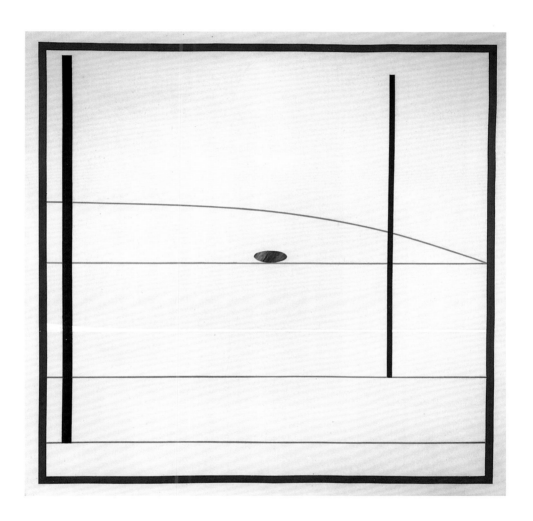

Temple garden

Temple avenue

four triangles

le jardin style information!

aves formes franche

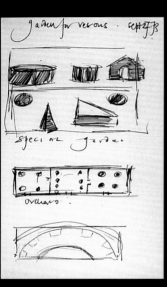

garden for vezons · sept 27 73

special garden

orchard.

1st draught   Derek Jarman   Louis XIII garden scene Sevis

first drawing sept 73.

a garden for the vezons herefordshire

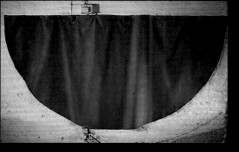

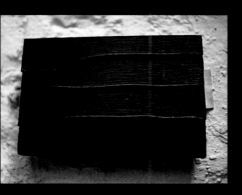

OPPOSITE
Top left: Studies for the garden at The Verzons,
(with special garden and orchard) from Notebook
C3C, September 1973
Top right: Two pages of studies for the garden at
The Verzons, from Notebook C3C, September 1973
Centre right: 'Louis XIII garden scene', design study
for *The Devils*, 1970
Bottom: 'A garden for The Verzons, Herefordshire',
September 1973

Above: *Untitled (Archer)*
Oil on canvas, 1983

OPPOSITE
Irresistible Grace
Oil on canvas, 1982

Derek Jarman: The Art of Films/Films of Art

Michael O'Pray, Reader in Visual Theories, University of East London

Norman Rosenthal, the curator and writer, remarked recently that he had always considered Derek Jarman a painter 'who from time to time makes films to surprise and entertain his friends'.[1] This view seems to upturn, somewhat ironically, Jarman's public image as a film-maker who dabbled now and then in painting. Of course, there is often a huge discrepancy between the public face and the private life, and in the last few years as Jarman's paintings have received more and more attention, there has been good reason to take Rosenthal's judgment of Jarman more seriously. There are definite connections to be made between his paintings and his film work, although what follows are more often than not suggestions, impressions and possible lines for future research.

Two distinct modes of relationship can be discerned between his films and paintings. On the one hand, some of the films share subject matter and form with the paintings. This is specially true of both the Super 8 films of the 1970s and early 1980s. On the other hand, many of his films take the painter, and more broadly speaking the artistic creator, as a central figure, e.g. *Caravaggio* (1986), *Imagining October* (1984), *The Tempest* (1979), *War Requiem* (1989) and, perhaps more tenuously, *Jubilee* (1978). A third relationship that needs mentioning is one which concerns the art process itself. Unlike many of his peers, Jarman made films rather as one makes paintings. To recognize this is to understand films like *In the Shadow of the Sun* (1974–80), *The Angelic Conversation* (1985) and *The Last of England* (1987) whose raw power, fragmentary style, textured images, sprawling narrative and bricolage-like forms suggest a painterly approach to film. Jarman compared film to the 'rough edges' made by the Japanese potter who 'has turned a perfect tea bowl and then jabs it with his thumb, sending ripples through the work'.[2]

Jarman attended the Slade as a painter in the mid-1960s, although he spent much time in theatre design where he experienced a more relaxed attitude to homosexuality.[3] Befriending Patrick Procktor, he quickly became a member of the circle around the Pop artist David Hockney. After exhibiting theatrical designs at the Biennale des Jeunes in Paris in 1967, he was commissioned to design Frederick Ashton's ballet *Jazz Calendar* in 1968 and, later the same year, to design John Gielgud's production of *Don Giovanni*. He remarked '[T]he beginning of my career was to resemble the end of anyone else's'.[4] Having

Punks outside the Kebab House in Jubilee, 1978

exhibited his paintings at the Lisson Gallery in 1967 and later in 1969, he highlighted 'the division that was opening up in my work between the painter and the designer'.[5] This division was to become even wider when, in the doldrums and somewhat disillusioned with his theatre work, he decided to accept Ken Russell's offer to be production designer on his controversial film *The Devils* in 1970. In fact, in *Dancing Ledge* he traces his disillusionment with painting, which he found 'undemanding' and 'enervating',[6] to this exhausting but exhilarating year working with Russell. However, he does admit continuing to paint during the 1970s, even if only 'sporadically'.

Shortly after becoming involved with *The Devils* he had acquired a Super 8 camera with which he made an enormous number of films – some staged and designed (*Tarot*, 1973; *The Art of Mirrors*, 1973), others of landscapes (*Journey to Avebury*, 1971), and others of friends and their surroundings (*Andrew Logan Kisses the Glitterati*, 1972; *Duggie Fields*, 1974; *Gerald's Film*, 1976). Undoubtedly the Super 8 films replaced the paintings as an expressive means during the first part of the 1970s. The camera's lightness, its unfussy loading mechanisms (a cassette) and cheapness allowed Jarman to work quickly and intuitively in ways akin to painting itself. He was able to explore formal techniques, especially superimposition and refilming at different speeds, achieved by the most primitive means.[7] Film was also conducive to developing subject matter around his interests in alchemical and cabbalist symbolism and ritual.

Jarman's paintings in the late 1960s were cool, minimal, spacious works often dealing with landscape as in *Cool Waters* (1965), with its de Chirico feel (p. 57), and the extremely minimal but spatial landscape painting shown in *Dancing Ledge*.[8] The film equivalent of these paintings is *The Art of Mirrors*[9] with its bare extended foreground and background wall often about two thirds of the way up the frame (the camera moves backwards and forwards, adjusting this line). The three figures are mysterious – in one case hooded – and posed quite deliberately in this space, one often in the foreground and the two others in the background. Their movement is stylized and slowed down, encouraging an awareness of the camera as a framing device. The film has an elegant, abstracted and ritualistic atmosphere, with the light reflected into the camera lens achieving a purely filmic effect of casting the image into negative.

In Jarman's film *Journey to Avebury* there is a similar use of long-shot of the landscape, again emphasizing the line of the horizon and the deep extended foreground, but the image does not itself have any of the worked-over painterly feel gained by refilming. The connections are more literal: in the 'Avebury' series of paintings made around the same time, one can see Jarman using the same source for the paintings and films. On this evidence, Jarman's claim to have given up painting seems most likely to mean that he had given up a certain commitment to his painting. As the 'Avebury' series reveals, he was painting during an extremely prolific film-making period between 1971 and 1975 before his energies were taken up by the feature films. It is also interesting that according to Jarman's notes and other sources, he was working on a series of 'landscape' films during the early to mid-70s.[10] It was a genre which he always valued, and landscape featured regularly in his work.

His introduction to feature-film making was as fortuitous as that to his Super 8 film work. A meeting in January 1975 with James Whaley led to *Sebastiane*. At the time of this meeting, Jarman had many projects planned. His notebooks are filled with scripts, ideas, sketches and lists of films, some of which never saw the light of day whilst others were cannibalized for later

Jordan as Amyl in *Jubilee*, 1978

67

The nurse (Tilda Swinton) with the body of Wilfred Owen (Nathaniel Parker), *War Requiem*, 1989

projects. For example, a script based on the early Elizabethan alchemist John Dee found its way into the punk classic *Jubilee* (1978).[11] The three feature films of the 1970s were all quite different. *Sebastiane* (1976), shot in the harsh relentless Mediterranean light, depicts an isolated 'hero', tortured and finally executed by his fellow soldiers, who pass their time in sexual trysts, cruel games and horseplay. This is to be contrasted with *Jubilee*'s futurist gang of anarchists, sex fiends, sado-masochists, pyromaniacs and its 'no-future' philosophy. Set in a decaying, wrecked London, the film's 'heroine' is Queen Elizabeth I, who is transported magically to witness the reign of her namesake. *The Tempest* (1979), on the other hand, is shot almost entirely in the flickering shadows of a large English country house. An adaptation of Shakespeare's play, it is more inward-looking, ethereal and rich in design and fantasy (pp. 76, 79, 98–9).

There is no direct equivalence in the paintings, it would seem. The painterly qualities of the Super 8 were replaced by the crystal-clear solidity of 16 mm and larger production values. But the features represent the beginnings of Jarman's exploration of the artist in society, an interest he shares with Ken Russell. In *Jubilee* and *The Tempest*, especially, Jarman deals with seers and visionaries. Elizabeth I is our guide through the apocalyptic landscape of England. And Prospero has always been identified with Shakespeare himself, performing his last artistic 'tricks' for his public. Both seers are also healers: the Queen and Prospero are keen to make things better in their Kingdoms, the former even if only in her sympathies, for her vision is in the future, whilst Prospero's actions – of reparation and of forgiveness – take place in the present. Many of Jarman's films contain this theme of the seer as emotional mediator of fragmenting, repressively cruel worlds. In *Caravaggio, The Last of England, War Requiem, The Garden* and *Blue*, there is a strong sense of creative figures or their equivalents attempting to give shape and some kind of balm to turbulent, dark, bleak times. For Jarman, the artist was always identified with this kind of visionary whose magic was equivalent to the procedures of art itself. Art was alchemy.

In 1982 Jarman had a painting show at the Edward Totah gallery.[12] He described the event as a 'damp squib'. The works 'drew on the fragments of Heraclitus, the technical drawing of Robert Fludd, Athanasius Kircher and seventeenth-century hermeticism'.[13] The show was called *After the Final Academy* in reference to the event held by William S. Burroughs (with John Giorno and Brion Gysin and others) in London a few weeks earlier.

Many of the misgivings I felt about painting in the early seventies resurface in the wake of this disappointment…. No one remembers or mentions the Lisson shows. No one has paid the least attention to the films and their relation to the work. The art world exists in a vacuum.[14]

Jarman mentions a second group of paintings, 'deeply affected' by Caravaggio, which used gold ground and were 'based on nineteenth-century photographs of the male nude mixed with sexual and religious iconography, back-room paintings'.[15] This group includes such paintings as *Night Life* (1982). But by 1984, at the time of Jarman's ICA retrospective show, he was ready to assert that painting was as much 'a centre of his life' as film,[16] and that he had written his

Baby wrapped in tabloids, *The Last of England*, 1987

autobiographical book *Dancing Ledge* partly in order to make connections between his film and his art work. At the time, Jarman's paintings were not part of his public persona. The success of *Sebastiane* (1976), *Jubilee* (1978) and *The Tempest* (1979) and the often lurid publicity that attended it had placed him in the public eye as a film-maker. But Jarman had not made a feature film since *The Tempest* in 1979 and one supposes he now found time and perhaps the need to return in a more focused way to his painting.

Before the ICA show, Jarman embarked on some new paintings including the 'GBH' series. All of these paintings share a dark ethereal quality, although there seems to be a reticence about them, perhaps owing to their classical allusiveness. They stem very much from *The Tempest* in their colour and cultural reference points. In their use of the figure, they are similar to the Super 8 film he began working on in the summer of 1984. These short films of young men swimming, play-fighting and acting out rituals were to become *The Angelic Conversation* (1985), the images being set to Shakespeare's sonnets. In fact, when the BFI awarded him development money for the 'Caravaggio' project he immediately went out and shot more material in the belief that these Super 8 'home movies' would be his 'Caravaggio' film. He had intended to shoot it on Super 8 in this experimental poetic style but one of the conditions of BFI production money when it eventually came, was that the film was to be shot on 35 mm. He was never happy with the static and cumbersome nature of 35 mm.[17]

The dark shadows of the caves and golden light of the flares, the chiaroscuro enveloping the often classical poses of the young men's bodies in *The Angelic Conversation*, were redolent of the black and gold paintings of the same period, such as, for example, *Dead Souls Whisper* (1982) and *All we see asleep is sleep, all we see awake is death* (1983). The connection between the films and painting are quite apparent here. They share the same rather cold, even abstract eroticism in which the nude is framed by a *mise en scène* of antiquity obviously owing to Jarman's immersion in the sixteenth-century alchemists, with perhaps a nod towards William Blake. There is also a concomitant idealization of the male figure and a weary melancholia which pervades both the film and the paintings.

In contrast, his brilliant short film *Imagining October*, made slightly later (1984), and which again is closely related to the 'Caravaggio' project, tackles the business of painting itself, locating it in this case in an historical nexus, albeit an imaginative one. Shot in the USSR and in London on Super 8 and video, it is both a polemic against the Empire-building and repression of Eastern and Western blocs, as Jarman experienced these at the height of the Thatcher–Reagan 'romance', and an essay on the complex relationship between artist, model, State, representation, sexuality and eroticism, using the style of social realism. In a key scene, the Soviet soldiers eat and drink at a long table suggesting the Last Supper (Pasolini had already made the Gospel According to St Matthew into a homo-erotic film of the same title). They strip to the waist and are painted by John Watkiss in a social realist style. The close-ups of the brush working the paint on the palette, the silence of the studio and the sexual frisson between artist and models capture the complexity of this seemingly mundane situation. The brutality and good looks of these soldiers signals their roles as political signifiers and sexual objects.[18] In a similar fashion, *Caravaggio*

Spring shooting up in *The Last of England*, 1987

treats the painter as a conduit for both ruling-class pornography and Catholic ideology, but one which Jarman makes literally flesh in the studio scenes where the exchange of money is embedded in sexual exploitation too. The image of the artist as fatally compromised is a view that at times Jarman shared.[19]

Jarman spent a great amount of time scripting films. Draft after draft was written for the feature films like *Caravaggio* and *The Tempest*. However in *The Last of England* there is a strong sense of a working process that disobeys all the rules of narrative construction or, for that matter, the mannerisms of poetic fracturing. Rather like a sculpture, the film is hewn out of its own substance. It comprises disparate footage, some shot with other ideas in mind, other parts improvised, others planned and some of the camera work done by other artists. From this unwieldy material, Jarman shaped the film with great energy, but it bears all the marks of the struggle for control – a sign of great art in which, as Will Self remarks, '[Jarman] offered us a set of discursive and yet plangent images of our own divided nature'.[20]

During this period in the mid-1980s Jarman was working on collages using thick black paint and pitch into which he pressed objects – a bullet, a knife,

nails, pebbles, seashells (p. 24) – and glass broken with a hammer (p. 121).[21] These works were shown at the Tate Gallery when he was nominated for the Turner Prize in 1986, when he was already filming *The Last of England*. If the paintings of the early 1980s are imbued with an antiquity in which his meditations on the male form can find an expression, then the tar collages are a distinct move towards a more direct form of address, one that culls its material from popular culture and from his own experiences of film-making and of living on the Kent shoreline at Dungeness. The collages more often than not incorporate hand-written text which emphasizes the desire for direct communication and also suggests the influence of William Blake.

The Last of England and *The Garden* were two highly personal films made with a similar collagist sensibility. Images are drawn from classical art, pop videos, TV advertising and Jarman's own aesthetic. There is in both films a swirling violence and brutal confrontation with his subject-matter. In the way that the text is embedded in the paintings, so the words encountered in these two films are woven through voice-over into the elegiac music and sounds of the film's soundtrack. For the first time, in the films and paintings, the voice is intensely personal, with Jarman appearing in both films as the source of the visions. Similarly, in the paintings, Jarman's own presence is strongly felt through his use of found objects from the nearby beach and subjective diary-like texts (see *5.30*, 1988).

In 1989 Jarman decided to stop collaging and return to painting. Although there is still a use of collage and text, these elements are much more integrated into the painted surface, so that it is less like a private diary, but rather a more public expression of admonitions, cries, exclamations of pain, polemics and, of course, wit. The paintings of the 1990s, many on a larger scale, are often densely textured and free in gesture. There is a tension between abstraction and the precision of language in works like *Ataxia* (1993) and *Death* (1993). In Jarman's final film *Blue* (1993), inspired by the work of Yves Klein, there is the same tension between the minimalist blue screen and the density of sounds accompanying this image. In *Blue*, he manages to bring together the collagist impulse – juxtaposing different kinds of voice from the personal to the philosophical with music, noises and sounds and the ominous abstraction of the saturated blue screen. It is as if a cacophony of sounds has supplanted the pandemonium of images.

In the narrative films *Edward II* (1991) and *Wittgenstein* (1992) Jarman explored repressed forms of homosexuality. His reworking of Marlowe's masterpiece resulted in an angry film which attacks the Establishment, past and present, for its illiberal attitudes and suggests that political power perhaps always

The boys on the beach, *The Garden,* **1990**

Steven Waddington (King Edward) and Andrew Tiernan (Piers Gaveston), *Edward II*, 1991

corrupts, as he had felt when making *The Tempest* many years earlier. In its theme and mood, it is very much in keeping with the paintings of the time. Although he had been drawn to the philosopher Wittgenstein some years earlier as a possible subject for a film, the tone is calmer and more stoical in the film he was commissioned to make about him. Wittgenstein's intensely ambivalent and warring nature between a cold, abstract philosophical system and a Romantic passion perhaps reflected Jarman's own restlessness. It also offered him a model for life and death, one in which personal struggle, and the lack of resolution in matters of sexuality could be seen in a positive light. *Wittgenstein* and *Edward* both use pared down, minimalist sets and in the case of the former, strong primary colours. The sombre tones of the earlier films were banished as Jarman rediscovered the yellows and reds in his paintings as well. These late films are tightly constructed in a way quite different to the late expressionist paintings with their free flowing lines and exuberant splashes of colour. This perhaps reflects the inevitable constrictions of fairly large-scale feature-film making in comparison with the freedom of painting. But the films and the paintings hold in common a response to death. Jarman portrays Edward and

Wittgenstein as people who face death after lives of conflict between their desires and their responsibilities, something Jarman felt too. On the other hand, Jarman's last paintings, unburdened by the demands of narrative, of piecing things together, can respond intuitively to death with an enormous courage, openness and passion for life itself. And, supremely, at the core of both films and the paintings is the sheer urge to communicate, a rare quality in contemporary art.

1   Norman Rosenthal in *Derek Jarman Queer* (exhibition catalogue), Manchester City Art Galleries with Richard Salmon Ltd., 1992 np.

2   Derek Jarman, *War Requiem: The Film*, Faber and Faber, London, 1989, p. 47.

3   Derek Jarman, *Dancing Ledge*, Quartet Books, London, 1984, p. 67.

4   *Ibid*. p. 75.

5   *Ibid*. p. 74.

6   *Ibid*. p. 105.

7   Professional superimposition is done with an optical printer but Jarman projected the images onto a wall and then refilmed the resulting overlapping images. This does lead to some degrading of the image, lending it a coarser, almost painterly texture.

8   *Dancing Ledge*, p. 89.

9   'The Art of Mirrors' during the 1970s was the generic title for a series of films. I refer to the film that is now known by that title.

10 Jarman describes this series in an application to the Arts Council of Great Britain probably dated 18 April 1975. See my book *Derek Jarman: Dreams of England*, British Film Institute, London, 1996.

11 *Dancing Ledge*, p. 168.

12 *Ibid*. p. 228.

13 *Ibid*. p. 229.

14 *Ibid*. p. 228.

15 *Ibid*. p. 229.

16 *Square Peg* no. 4, 1984, p. 22.

17 'Brittania on Trial: Interview with Derek Jarman', *Monthly Film Bulletin,* vol. 53, no. 627, April 1986.

18 For example, compare Charles Jagger's Hyde Park war memorial bronzes which have a similar approach to masculinity. See *Charles Sargeant Jagger: War and Peace Sculpture*, ed. Ann Compton, Imperial War Museum, London, 1985.

19 Interview in *Afterimage* no. 12 Autumn 1985 p. 46; *Dancing Ledge*, p. 235.

20 Will Self, 'Birth of the Cool', *The Guardian Weekend*, August 6, 1994, pp. 27–28.

21 For further examples of this work see *Luminous Darkness*, Uplink, Tokyo, 1990.

The 'fabric of this vision': designing *The Tempest* with Derek Jarman

Yolanda Sonnabend, artist and stage designer

Derek and I had both been theatre design students under Robert Medley at the Slade and Robert became, for both of us, a lasting friend and influence. We showed our designs together at the Paris Biennale in 1967 and I was always aware of Derek's activities. Among his various and multiple creative expressions were exhilarating parties, reflected light and magic in the Butler's Wharf setting: waitresses served in backless gowns, the piano sounded the odd nocturne, Frederick Ashton and Robert Medley playing extravagant charades. In my mind I recall this masque-like levity. We lived in Derek's persuasive fantasy which he distilled like a necromancer. He knew how to create an occasion and, in a sense, created the occasion for the film of *The Tempest*. Some of the ingredients matched – Stoneleigh Abbey (the house was even historically related to *The Tempest*); poets, artists, dwarves and guests; corridors and empty rooms to dream in. A setting for a great party.

When Derek asked me to design *The Tempest*, I was delighted. Derek of course could have done it himself, but he enjoyed the collaboration to the extent that he would attribute the work to you, even if it was for his inventions. Initially I wasn't clear about my part. Derek's visions were always larger than reality. I started to make a model of the great room at Stoneleigh, with its rows of windows, through which to film the sea crashing, but that disappeared. As the film progressed we all designed parts of the settings, happy to share our talents. I had occasional regrets when ideas were dismissed. Miranda had a vicious, chattering, articulated little beast she wore on her shoulder, a monkey cat exquisitely fashioned by Christopher Hobbs – I never understood its going. For the ball sequence I gathered all my students and random helpers to fabricate what seemed like miles of garlands, an imaginary 'salle fleurie'. Everybody helped. In the Trinculo–Stephano–Ariel scene, the monsters were assembled ad hoc from what I had around, though I attempted a giant de Chirico figure of velvet and cement which didn't work. But the costumes slid my way. Derek joined in all the time. We combed markets together foraging for the right sublime material: for Miranda we found a train of gossamer silk embroidered with blue beads to throw over her crinoline, and for her scenes as a child (when she was played by his niece) some rare flowery satin (p. 98).

Miranda (Toyah Wilcox) and Ferdinand (David Meyer) in *The Tempest*, 1979

We would vandalize; I was hesitant, but Derek conjured up Diaghilev, who habitually raided raiments and tore them up for the Russian ballet, the end justifying the means. Derek's ideas were often brilliant and overflowing; he seemed entranced and enchanted, but in this whirlpool ideas came and went. The glittering diamond-studded sneakers for Ariel were rejected, compensated for by a pair of lyrical, gem-embroidered shoes for Miranda.

Memories of making the costumes are still vivid, perhaps because they were a pleasure to do. As their project, Wimbledon School of Art costume department, under Michael Pope, made a perfect replica of a crinoline with every eyelet detail. The bodice was covered with shredded satin, embellished with shells, feathers and island treasures. At one point the crinoline was about to be rejected, and I tore down to Stoneleigh to rescue it. The swaying mattered as much as the froth. It was saved. Miranda's ball dress was another bizarre concoction. A heady Hollywood fourteenth century, it nonetheless had a certain unity. Derek was ahead of his time. It is fashionable now to combine periods, psychologically and sartorially; Derek anticipated this.

There were so many details. Derek cherished the memory of a fan seen in an attic when he was a child, perhaps in Rome. He described a ring of black birds' beaks studded with aquamarine eyes. We made one but it was never used. How could it recreate such a memory? Instead he found a battered ivory fan in my drawer for Miranda to peer through. Elizabeth Welch (our Juno) was an Inigo Jones creation filtered through the movies. She was superb at handling costume. I presented her with gold chains and she quickly slithered them through her fingers. Derek sensed and knew all about that kind of performer's artistry.

The dwarves became my special concern – part of the court of the film and part of our own court. At first Derek wanted a midget. A midget arrived, smoking a cigar, but was too costly, so the dwarves entered. One was pensive and gentle, who would wander off, feeding the swans in the idyllic landscape, the other strong and more aggressive (I think she had a rock band and might have been the daughter of a general). Both inspired me to paint their portraits. They were mirror images, one light, one dark. Again Wimbledon School of Art, under Jane Curwood, made them neo-Velazquezes, covered in tinkles and bells, pampered and shimmering little figures (p. 98). I painted their hands with glitter. Derek taught me about shine, about sequins and light illuminating a costume. As the woman on set I occasionally had to attend to rather intimate details of costuming – arranging a bouquet of leaves on Sycorax's private parts, for instance. I never knew whether this was a barely visible token ornament or prudish cover.

And if the costumes, always with Derek at hand, inhabit my mind, so do the rooms. I can still wander through Stoneleigh as it was, grand, stuccoed and fire-ruined. It even had a chapel, as every court should, and there was naturally a haunted brown and gold room (which I turned into a painting).

But the presiding magus, was Derek, lifting everybody with his enthusiasm. Everybody worked hard but, at least it seemed to me, without strain. We followed. I remember Prospero's study for the first time. Simon Read drew the mysterious neo-Platonic scribbles and the floor was a formation of candles. Rudolphian images, and then the delight of the sailors' dance, where Stewart Hopps genially made even the most awkward into reelers.

If we worked hard, but not demonically, the evenings were for fun. Jack Birkett and Heathcote Williams entertained us, as poets and artists. In my memory work was always punctuated by parties orchestrated by Derek. We all wanted to go on living there, take it over, share it. We didn't want to let it go.

Like the dream of *The Tempest*, work and life were suspended. Derek, our Prospero, pulling the threads together, making us all willing conspirators in his vision. Some celestial harmony breathed on us for a while. He said films were not always like this. It was hardly a commercial venture, more like an adventure of the spirit. Full of love, hope and gaiety. A young man's film of an old man's thoughts.

Elizabeth Welch, *The Tempest*, 1979

theatre opening

Designing for the Theatre and Cinema

Peter Snow, Professor of Theatre Design, Slade School of Art

It is difficult to write about any aspect of Derek Jarman's considerable talent without acknowledging his generous and courageous character. Humanity, wit, wry defiance and imagination, fused with kindness and plain common sense informed every part of his work and personality.

I first remember him when I came to teach at the Department of Theatre Design at the Slade School of Art in the early 1960s. He was a young student there, and claimed then, perhaps tongue in cheek, then that he had entered as a refugee from the Painting Department, finding the liberal ambience sympathetic. He was one of those heaven-sent students: curious, energetic and almost entirely self-motivated. I think it would be fair now to concede that his quick intelligence led to a positive collaborative association, rather than a pupil-teacher relationship, but there was no arrogance or cockiness about him. His enthusiasm for learning was a delight. He was as eager for knowledge at the end of a class as at the beginning.

Influenced by the contemporary American artist Robert Rauschenberg's 'Dante Suite' and by the English Pop painter Richard Hamilton, he devised an original scale model for Stravinsky's dramatic oratorio *Orpheus*, made up from collages cut out of male muscle magazines. The design caused some uneasiness from the Slade Professor, Sir William Coldstream. Coldstream had written a letter, together with a number of establishment academics, in defence of the integrity and responsibility of homosexual artists in society (he was a lifelong friend of W. H. Auden), and he showed initial nervousness at Jarman's open images. Fortunately his admonishments, probably half in jest, had little effect. Coldstream himself, the most subtle and civilized of administrators, would probably not have been shocked.

Jarman's next design model project was for *Huis Clos* by Jean-Paul Sartre, the set covered entirely in red velvet, with three armchairs in yellow, blue and black (p. 92). That term the class was studying Jonson's *Volpone*. For this, perhaps remembering the earlier encouragement of his art master Robin Noscoe at Canford School, who had a passion for silversmithing, he produced a scale model of the old Fox's lair, cluttered with cupboards stuffed full of gold and treasure which he had hoarded. It was exquisitely fashioned, as by some ingenious oriental craftsman. Goblets, jewelry, vases and statues spilled out onto

and under the large damascene bed in the centre of the stage, in a rich metaphor of secret, gilded avarice.

Jarman commenced his career at the Slade as a painter, which his RAF father supported once he had studied English, History and the History of Art (which included Architecture under Nikolaus Pevsner) at King's College, London. There he had been awarded first prize for amateurs at the University of London Union – *Daily Express* Art Exhibition in 1961. The composition award for professionals went to a young David Hockney at the Royal College of Art. Subsequently the two students became friends and rivals, Hockney later contributing to the theatre as well as painting. Jarman admired Hockney's bleached hair, neon socks and New York lifestyle, while remaining himself resolutely English.

Like Philip Prowse, who had already left the Slade some years before him, eventually becoming the distinguished Director-Designer of the Citizen's Theatre, Glasgow, Jarman already recognized the direction of his own talent while still a student. Future years were to witness the fulfilment of it. He began precociously at the Slade by exhibiting his theatre designs for Prokofiev's *The Prodigal Son* at the 1967 Biennale des Jeunes Artistes in Paris (p. 92), then won a prestigious Peter Stuyvesant Award for Painting at the *Young Contemporaries* at the Tate Gallery in May the same year.

His concern for images in the theatre or cinema always remained that of a painter. Jarman continued to paint throughout his career, encouraged by the guru artist Robert Medley, and by Nicholas Logsdail, an enterprising fellow student, also from the department, who, with his wife Fiona, opened the Lisson Gallery in an old shop in Paddington, specializing in conceptual non-figurative art. The first exhibition, a group show, somewhat misleadingly titled *English Twentieth Century Landscape*, included work by Jarman and was followed by a show with his friend and associate Keith Milow.

He showed at a number of other galleries including that of Edward Totah, the ICA and, towards the end of his life, at the fashionable Karsten Schubert Gallery, then in Charlotte Street. The last of these were mostly large expressionist canvases, which he completed in some pain. These were raw, violent, frightening, abstract pictures, protesting his outrage at the disease which was threatening him. It was the only time I felt Derek's bitterness and frustration. His published diary rarely gives vent to such fury or despair.

Jarman was shrewd enough to recognize early on in his innovative career how important Fine Art was to him. He travelled extensively in Europe, America and Russia. He was widely and deeply informed about the art and architecture of the past, keen to see and find out as much as he could about the most contemporary movements. It was no wonder, therefore, that his enthusiasm as a creative artist embraced, amongst others, the genius of Jean Cocteau, Kenneth Anger, Vladimir Mayakovsky, Sergei Eisenstein, Pier Paolo Pasolini, Federico Fellini, Pablo Picasso and William S. Burroughs as well as Caravaggio. Jarman's travels were often made in impecunious and uncomfortable circumstances, but he was equally at home at all levels of society, mixing unobtrusively and roughing it when necessary.

These experiences stood him in good stead all his life, whether designing for the theatre, writing his diaries, or as a cinema *auteur*. Jarman became a genuine 'culture punk', although meeting and talking to him, one was aware only that he was, as Nicholas de Jongh said, a gentleman.

As a student of history and literature at King's College, Jarman thought *visually*, and at the Slade, as a painter, he continued his fascination with literature and history. He must have been one of the most well read and literate students of his generation. But at all times he was concerned with the human condition and its contradictory nature. His film of Britten's *War Requiem* portrayed its misery; Elizabeth Welch, singing in *The Tempest*, the joy. His reworking of *The Tempest* in 1979

Above: The hawk and a monstrous figure in the dress rehearsal of *Throughway* for Ballet Rambert, 3 March 1968
Below: Jarman fitting a mask for a performance event in the late 1960s (perhaps 'The Synthetic Cubist', autumn 1968)

OPPOSITE
Slade Theatre Design projects: Prokofiev's ballet *The Prodigal Son*, summer 1967, 'Home' (top) and the journey Scene (middle); Ben Jonson's *Volpone*, 1966 (bottom)

Dress rehearsal for *Jazz Calendar*, Royal Ballet, Covent Garden, London, 8 January 1968

was a revelation of Shakespeare and of the 'magick' of Prospero–Dr Dee: his power, eventual resignation and forgiveness.

Although basically a solitary man, living happily with his loyal companion Keith, returning from excursions to London, Berlin and New York back home to his cottage in Dungeness, he was paradoxically the most gregarious of artists. He *loved* people – a tendency which led him occasionally into danger, as well as into convivial company. Ironically, as in Wilde's *Ballad of Reading Gaol*, this love eventually took its unfair revenge on him. Derek like being alone, but he dreaded being lonely. Not to be invited to a party to which 'everyone else was going' filled him with melancholy. He was like the character Elliot Templeton, brilliantly played by the late Clifton Webb in Somerset Maugham's film *The Razor's Edge*. To be left off the invitation list was really unbearable – though having been asked, he did not necessarily turn up.

Happily, however, Jarman was entirely without exclusivity or snobbishness. His talent, rather than keeping itself to itself, was freely given. As he said himself, he was unable to keep secrets. It was the encouragement, help and hope that he extended to others which set him especially apart from his contemporaries: creativity shared. Many younger and older people benefited from working with him, though regrettably some were nervous of being associated with his open homosexuality, fearing their own careers might be compromised. Those who did, however, included many distinguished actors such as Laurence Olivier, Ian Charleson, Michael Gough, Peter Bull, Richard O'Brien, Jenny Runacre and the iconic Tilda Swinton, the poet Heathcote Williams, pop stars Toyah Wilcox and Adam Ant, painters Robert Medley, Yolanda Sonnabend and Patrick Procktor, mime artists Lindsay Kemp with Orlando and company, media artists and sculptors Peter and Andrew Logan, Christopher Hobbs and many friends who freely gave their affection and time.

In 1968, Sir Frederick Ashton, the choreographer-director of the Royal Ballet, engaged Jarman to design the ballet *Jazz Calendar* for the Royal Opera House (p. 89). With music by Richard Rodney Bennett, the ballet was to be danced by the Company, with the fiercely intimidating and temperamental Rudolf Nureyev, who continually complained about his costume, ridiculing it mercilessly in front of the whole Company until the first night when, to Derek's relief, he finally appeared on stage wearing it. Overcoming prejudices concerning age and experience, Jarman used a firm political charm, and succeeded in getting his way with the setting. The ballet was a triumph (it has recently been revived by the Royal Ballet in Birmingham, under the enterprising Sir Peter Wright).

Later in the same year, John Gielgud asked Jarman to design Mozart's *Don Giovanni* for English National Opera, with which it was planned to open at their new home at the Coliseum in London. Jarman, who much admired the work of Duchamp, de Chirico and the Cubists, invented a number of geometrical sets using his own interpretations of theatrical cubism and structuralism, inspired by Picasso's designs for *Le Tricorne* (pp. 90–1). Though these would certainly be found acceptable and even thrilling today, especially after the popular creative regime of David Pountney in the 1980s and early 1990s at the English National Opera, the public was scandalized and refused to make sense of the conceptual connections. The first night, which I attended, was a disaster. Opera critics, like some ballet critics, are not perhaps always known for their ready acceptance or even serious consideration of new visual interpretations. Gielgud's production and Jarman's designs were unfairly savaged at the time.

At the end of his time at the Slade, Jarman's work was 'discovered' by Ken Russell, who had been introduced to him by Janet Deueter. In 1970, Russell, himself a film-maker with a strong and independent visual

Jarman's set for *The Devils*, 1970

The Rake's house (above) and Angel underground station (opposite) in *The Rake's Progress*, 1982

sense, commissioned Jarman as production designer for his first film *The Devils*, an adaptation of a successful stage play by John Whiting, which had recently been performed at the Aldwych Theatre by the Royal Shakespeare Company. Jarman responded to this with some immense, early postmodernist sets (several of which had to be abandoned because of their size and cost). These were made of white bricks inspired by the silent Hollywood movies *Intolerance* and *Ben Hur*, and perhaps also by the yellow brick road in *The Wizard of Oz*, a favourite of his (pp. 85, 96). It is likely, too, that he had seen the white set designed by Sally Jacobs for the Peter Brook production of *The Marat/Sade*. He based his giant figure of Christ on Grünewald's Isenheim altarpiece, which made an indelible impression on him during a student visit to Colmar. *The Devils* was a heady mixture of Catholic and Calvinist sadomasochism and guilt, with memorable performances from Vanessa Redgrave, Oliver Reed and Max Adrian.

It was such a success that a year later, in 1971, Russell commissioned Jarman to work on his next film, *Savage Messiah*, based on the short life of the sculptor Henri Gaudier-Brzeska, who was killed in the trenches in 1915 at the age of twenty-three. The budget, funded by Russell himself, was tight, but what was lacking in finance was made up for by much ingenuity and imagination. Lively sculptures were carved and copies made of Gaudier-Brzeska's drawings and of his Omega furniture – much of these were apparently indistinguishable from the originals.

Despite the failure of Gielgud's *Don Giovanni* in 1968, the London Festival Ballet, directed by Beryl Grey, commissioned Jarman in September 1973 to design a new dance with the choreographer Tim Spain, to be called *Silver Apples of the Moon* (p. 94). Reading a nerve-racking account of the production's gestation and its first and final night in Oxford leads me to regret that English Puritanism caused its suppression. Whether it was because the dancers wore flesh-coloured tights or spectacles with primary-coloured tutus, or both, I have not discovered. It was reported that Beryl Grey was so shocked that it was never to appear again, remaining a whisper of imaginative designing. It reinforced, however, Derek's disillusionment with the theatre.

He created little more in the theatre after that, except for the loyal Ken Russell, who directed Stravinsky's *The Rake's Progress* at the Pergola Theatre in Florence in May 1982 (p. 28). It had to be designed and completed within ten days – a formidable artistic and practical assignment. The inspiration for the *Rake*'s hurried designs was punk–postmodernism. The settings were updated from the eighteenth century of Hogarth and Gay to contemporary London. There were sympathetic parallels to Stravinsky's own neo-classical music, and to the Kallman-Auden libretto, though the critics predictably questioned his interpretation of the composer's nostalgia for the period. This time, however, except for problems with the making of the design, due to pressure of time, few compromises were made, which pleased Russell, Jarman, and, thankfully, the

Italian public, who rewarded the production with a resounding box-office success. In 1988 he returned to Italy to direct Sylvano Bussotti's *L'Ispirazione* for the Maggio Musicale.

This was almost to be Jarman's swansong in the theatre. Asked to design a new production of Samuel Beckett's *Waiting for Godot* with the comedians Rick Mayall and Adrian Edmondson at the Queen's Theatre, London, he chose a promising theatre design graduate from the Slade, Madeleine Morris, to collaborate with him on the set. He also worked on a minuscule production of Jean Genet's *The Maids*, mounted at the nightclub 'Heaven'. The actresses were Tania and Michele Wade, who run the legendary Maison Bertaux in Soho.

It is ironic, but not surprising in retrospect, that Jarman's postmodernist ideas have since become a contemporary visual language in the theatre. There is no 'authentic' design for the theatre which lasts forever. Theatre must forever re-invent itself in order to mirror society. Jarman's work in theatre design played with the notion of historical authenticity while always concentrating on the social aspects treated by the work itself. The most original English designers and directors have used this style in many successful recent productions, among them Richard Jones, Tom Cairns, David Fielding, David Ultz, at the Royal Court under Stephen Daldry, the RSC, the Old Vic (during Jonathan Miller's short but innovative reign) and eventually at the Royal Opera House and the National Theatre led by Richard Eyre. Jarman was ahead of his time.

His last moving gesture was in the film *Blue*, whose only image on the screen was an unchanging projection of the same shade of blue (p. 160). It could be said to have resembled a painted backdrop, against which his frustration and laughter became a reconciliation to his own death. *Blue*, he said, 'transcends the geography of human limits'. In some ways the film represents a synthesis of all his work, in which the strands of his genius – painting, diary-writing, designing, film-making – were finally woven together, and in which at the same time he acknowledges Yves Klein and Kazimir Malevich; I consider it his most important and personal work. The purity and abstraction of the blue screen brings to our experience of the colour a sense of magic, even intoxication. Here, too, the paradoxes of his personality assumed a terrible logic. Pain became grace, agony became love. Like the flowers he tended so patiently and hopefully in his garden, against the salt spray, the wind, the gales and the threatening nuclear reactor, the seeds he sowed have finally taken root.

Jazz Calendar 1968, Royal Ballet, Covent Garden, London
Above: Set design for the '7 Day Finale'
Below: Thursday ('Far to go'), dress rehearsal, 8 January 1968

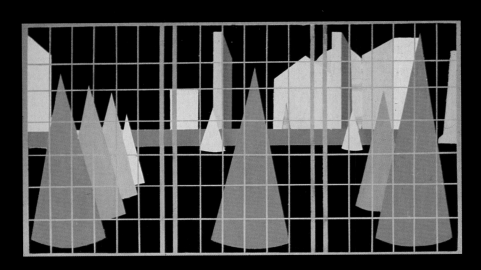

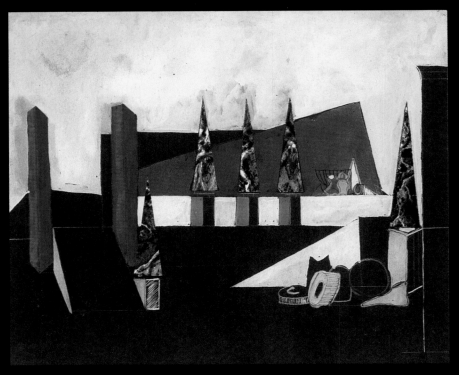

Street scene from *Don Giovanni* dress rehearsal, English
National Opera, Coliseum, London, August 1968

OPPOSITE
Above: Design for garden scene stage cloth for *Don Giovanni*,
English National Opera, Coliseum, London, 1968
Below: Preliminary study for *Don Giovanni*, April 1968

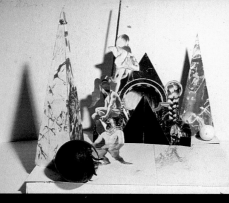

Four Slade Theatre Design projects
Top left: the orgy scene in Prokofiev's ballet *The Prodigal Son*, summer 1967
('perhaps the best thing in its section' at the 1967 Paris Biennale des Jeunes Artistes,
The Times)
Top right: entrance to the underworld in *Orpheus*, summer 1966
Bottom left: Jonson's *Volpone*, summer 1966
Bottom right: Sartre's *Huis Clos*, summer 1967

Dress rehearsal of *Throughway* for Ballet Rambert,
3 March 1968: the fight after the tea party with the monstrous
figures, as the hawk looks on

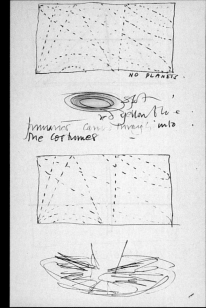

Above left: *The Beach*, with Slade students and Yolanda Sonnabend at the Collegiate Theatre, London, 12 June 1969
Above right: Studies for lighting in *Silver Apples of the Moon*, for London Festival Ballet, 1973
Below: *Mouth of the Night* for Mantis Dance Company, 1985:
'a large human body falling on one side, grim skull on the other, and Munch-like nudes across a superb backcloth, fronted by an altar-cum-wreath' *Sunday Telegraph* 17 February 1985

The Maids designed by Jarman with Nicole Robinson, 1992 (top and bottom).
'Derek Jarman's boudoir – festoons of white lace and swathes of gladioli – is paired with a sci-fi
bank of TVs left above-stage…' *City Limits* 21–28 January 1993

Above: Jarman's design for
the Church Square in Loudon,
The Devils, 1970
Right: Script for 'Dr Dee –
the Art of Mirrors and
a Summoning of Angels',
notebook A5, October 1975

OPPOSITE
Stills from Super 8 films
Above: *Journey to Avebury* 1971–72
Centre: *Art of Mirrors* 1973
Below: *A Garden in Luxor* 1972

The Tempest, 1979
Left: one of the 'Velazquez' dwarves
Centre: Miranda as a child, with a rare
flowery satin costume
Right: Elizabeth Welch and sailors in
the finale

The Last of England, 1987
Adam Elliott (nude) and Rod Laye

OPPOSITE
The Garden, 1990

Caravaggio, 1986
Right: Page from a notebook for *Caravaggio*
Below: Ranuccio (Sean Bean) and his lover
Lena (Tilda Swinton) with Caravaggio (Nigel
Terry) painting *St John the Baptist*

OPPOSITE
Above: Dexter Fletcher as the young
Caravaggio in a *tableau vivant* based on
The Sick Bacchus
Below: Corner of the artist's studio

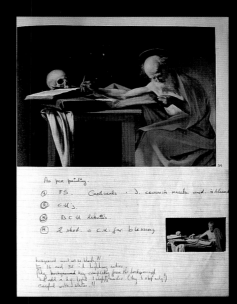

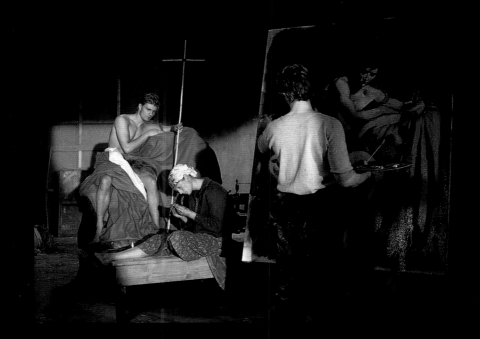

'Words written without any stopping':[1] Derek Jarman's Written Work

Matt Cook, social historian, at present working on sexuality and the city

*'It was very important to find the "I": I feel this, this happened to me, I did this.
I wanted to read that. My obsession with biography is to find these "I"s. The subtexts
of my films have been my books, putting myself back into the picture.'[2]*

Jarman's written output was large and diverse, ranging from poetry,
autobiography and annotated screenplays to a collection of thoughts on colour.
In all of it, as he suggests, he asserts his 'I' and marks out his perspective
determinedly and yet also draws on other texts, from the literary and biblical to
those of the media and advertising. This essay seeks to explore Jarman's use of
these diverse voices and his personal and political investment in writing and the
written word.

There is a sense throughout Jarman's work of a life never summed up but
constantly re-imagined. The prologue added to the 1991 edition of his first
autobiography, *Dancing Ledge*, originally published in 1984, is testament to this.
Under the heading 'A Footnote to My Past' he writes: 'The Years since
[*Dancing Ledge* was first published] have seen the renewal and reinvention of
my cinema…the reclaiming of the Queer past…my move to Prospect Cottage,
catching the virus and falling in love. …My body was thrown into the struggle,
bringing me into a spotlight I never expected or wanted'.[3]

The metaphorical, artistic and physical spaces he has moved onto are
profoundly different from those detailed in the main text. As his body enters
'the struggle' (implying both a medical and political fight) he is thrust into
a different cultural space, involving a new relationship with the surrounding
world. The authority and conclusive trajectory of classic autobiography, in which
the end of the text is also the end of a life worth documenting, are thus denied
at the very start of this edition of *Dancing Ledge*. Instead Jarman gestures to new
work, life and ambitions beyond not just the close of the book but also the end
of the added prologue: 'On 22 December 1986, finding I was body positive,
I set myself a target: I would disclose my secret and survive Margaret Thatcher.
I did. Now I have my sights on the millennium and a world where we are all
equal under the law.'[4]

The two subsequent autobiographies mark this re-invention, reworking the
past detailed in *Dancing Ledge* to support the new conditions of his life. Thus

Jarman writing *Chroma* at St Bartholomew's Hospital, London, mid-1992

Modern Nature (1991) centres largely on Dungeness and his garden, exploring a new temporal awareness that accompanied his diagnosis, as well as the altered stance of others towards him. The text is reflective, poetic and comes as an act of remembrance of his own life and mourning for others. *At Your Own Risk* (1992), meanwhile, abandons a day-by-day diary for an angry swipe at a generation of oppression. It is his testimony to Britain's endemic homophobia, and the inaction, silence and sometimes all too powerful voices that have characterized the response to HIV and AIDS. It takes remembrance and memory into angry activism.

One text does not pick up where the previous one left off but comes as a re-appraisal from a different position. Thus it does not invalidate what went before but asserts a voice that has moved on from, and yet also encompasses, the old. In each, for example, he writes about 'coming out', but the emphasis and terms of (self-) definition change. In *Dancing Ledge* he writes: 'After weeks of self-debate, I sat with [Roger] one evening and told him I was homosexual. I was terrified that this revelation might destroy our friendship';[5] in *Modern Nature*: 'I fell in love with a particularly charming theologian, Roger, and walked from Russell Square to Bethnal Green on several Sundays to see him. I eventually blurted out my dilemma over a cup of tea, didn't tell him he was the object of my desire – so our friendship continued';[6] and in *At Your Own Risk*: 'In that year I told Roger, one of the theologians, I thought I might be Queer. He reacted in a very affirmative way but offered no solution.... There was nothing much to go by'.[7]

The carefully pondered revelations in *Dancing Ledge* move to an anecdotal description of a clumsy, almost comic event in *Modern Nature*. The relationship with Roger is pivotal in both, and the event is of personal more than political significance. In *At Your Own Risk* this emphasis is reversed, and the event is reported factually to make a point. Jarman is now 'Queer', capitalized and politicized, not a clinically categorized 'homosexual'.

There is a sense here and elsewhere of writing being a means to self-mastery and knowledge for Jarman – he notes in *Dancing Ledge* 'you don't know what you have to say until you've said it'.[8] The corollary of this is a further feeling, particularly in his later work, of writing in order 'to be'. He configures himself in the pages of his published work and private diaries to assert his continued presence and voice, and to mark out his (changing) identity. It is both a personally empowering and politically powerful technique. He writes in *At Your Own Risk*: 'The problem of so much of the writing about the epidemic is the absence of the author.... It is no good alerting the "public" whilst distancing yourself.'[9]

Jarman's witnessing of the AIDS epidemic, his own illness and, crucially, responses to it, supersede a generalized rhetoric and isolate his voice. In this way he can indicate and begin to compensate for a chilling silence that has closed around a 'frosted generation',[10] and prevent it closing around him. His refusal to stop after the first autobiography and his determination to continue working keeps that space open and the voice alive. In this way the perceived chronology of HIV and AIDS and the supposed non-productive limbo of 'almost death'[11] once diagnosed are belied by his prolific output: 'they kept saying the film was my death film but I kept defying that'.[12]

'Putting [himself] back into the picture' in his work, importantly, also divests it of any claims to objectivity – what is produced is explicitly his arrangement and his perspective. He comments in *Queer Edward II* (1991): 'Social realism is as fictitious as the BBC news which has just one man's point of view. Like my film'.[13] He is acutely aware of the potential power of this 'point of view' once it is rendered in print or celluloid. He thus turns on texts and histories which masquerade as objective truth and so 'castrate our vibrant present'.[14] In *At Your Own Risk* he attacks 'the old moral proscriptions…put out by government and press aided and abetted by…Mary Whitehouse's flirtation with the corpse of nineteenth-century morality'.[15] The real pervert is exposed: a necrophiliac censor deeply enamoured of dead Victoriana. His talent, though, is not simply to attack but to engage actively in the oppressive rhetoric of certain dominant discourses. In *The Last of England* (1987) he comments: 'You can't leave the Bible in the hands of people like the Chief Constable of Manchester, God alone knows what he would do with it'.[16]

Rather than standing in direct opposition to the force which 'has formed the world in which we live' he 'embraces it'[17] in order to transgress its power more effectively. In *Modern Nature*, for example, holy days are marked in the diary format and a religious register is frequently invoked:

But I knew the joy of heaven was there, the splendour and nobility of warriors and I vowed to revenge my generations, to shred the false white veil of holy matrimony and fuck the haughty Groom, and to wipe his come with the Saviour's shroud. Then our task completed on earth we would enter the Kingdom, a band of warriors and gang-bang the Trinity on its throne of gold before a multitude of saints, until this Christ repented and confessed his true love of Saint John. Now and forever Amen.[18]

The language is familiar – 'joy', 'heaven', 'splendour', 'vow' – but its power is soon channelled into a violence against the institutions, systems and icons which have worked, or rather have been worked, to the exclusion of Jarman and his 'warriors'. Each lauded term is desecrated by a word preceding it, doing literary violence to it – the white veil is 'false' and 'shred(ded)', the Groom 'fuck(ed)', the Saviour's shroud come-stained, the Trinity 'gang-banged', and so on. Framed as a prayer it gains incantatory power, but Jarman characteristically subverts the form: he embraces the dominant (as it necessarily embraces him), and so draws the reader in, whilst using another discourse – that of the sexual vernacular – to attack its prescriptiveness. In this way the power of a dominant discourse and text (organized religion and the Bible) are harnessed to insist upon unenclosed and non-defined literary and filmic spaces from which to express and explore his own meanings and anger.

In *At Your Own Risk* these concerns gain further expression when Jarman both takes up and takes on the media. Quoting at length from Barbara Cartland's 1955 *Sunday Chronicle* article 'Destroy this evil', Jarman simply asks, 'Have times changed?'[19] He answers his own question some hundred pages later with the extended section of tabloid headlines, interspersed with 'another voice, the gay press'.[20] Jarman does not directly attack or support either 'voice' here, but by juxtaposing them he changes the signification of the former and emphasizes the necessity of the latter. Quoted in this way and in this context the headlines mutate to take on board Jarman's repulsion, as they do when daubed with red paint in his 'Queer' paintings (pp. 126–9). In the middle of this section is a set of photographs of Jarman and some friends – their lives not depicted by the media headlines that literally hem them in here. Through them he hints at the diversity that exists beyond the world of the straight press and registers a refusal to be constrained by its rhetoric. He thus draws us into his polemic, before turning his critique outwards. The section ends: 'And so it went as you hid behind the *Independent* and the *Guardian*, like those good Germans who never heard the windows smashing in the crystal night.'[21] Here is part of the need to continue writing – to counter not just homophobia but complacency. In a characteristic move the reader is jolted into a new position, from passive observer nodding agreement to 'victim' of a direct attack.

He uses literary texts and the 'biographies' of religious and artistic icons in a similar way, experimenting with different voices not to displace or distance his own but rather to position himself within, and to speak through, the culture which has produced and influenced him. Using these texts and figures invests his work with a wealth of existing meanings and associations. Reworking them, meanwhile, expands their story and store of meanings, which have often been pickled in a conventionalized telling. His aim is not to give them a definitive new meaning but to add other possibilities which speak to him and allow him to speak more directly. The construction of Caravaggio from his paintings, for example, certainly induces us to re-examine the artist, but the film and screenplay also draw us back to Jarman's own biography and agenda. He asserts that he and Caravaggio are 'both nocturnal backroom boys'[22] and notes elsewhere: 'The story, as it grew, allowed me to recreate many details of my own life, and, bridging the gap of centuries and cultures, to exchange the camera with a brush'.[23] There is an almost Romantic intermeshing of art with life here, with Caravaggio's relationship with his paintings 'reflecting' Jarman's with the film. It is a relationship he problematizes in the screenplay, yet it does demonstrate his personal investment in the work and his central position in its creation. This can be seen again in his portrayal of Sebastiane and in his film work with Shakespeare's sonnets and *The Tempest*. These figures and pieces clearly seize Jarman and by reframing them he brings forward 'the forebears who validated (his) existence'[24] and (self-consciously) makes them his own.

Our awareness of Jarman's agenda is possibly most acute in his work with Marlowe's *Edward II*. In it he does not attempt to reproduce an authentic history of the king (if such a thing were possible), but rather seeks to communicate his anger at the introduction of Clause 28 and the continued peddling of homophobic rhetoric in the late twentieth century. To this end Jarman ruthlessly cuts and re-arranges the play to shift its axis so that it turns almost exclusively on sexuality. It is the love affair between Edward and Gaveston which textures and motivates Jarman's screenplay, whereas it is arguably of secondary importance in the 'original'. Thus, whilst in Marlowe's treatment Edward achieves true majesty only once deposed and in prison, here it is with Gaveston, bathed in light. Jarman's construction of the story validates neither Marlowe's history of Edward nor his own, but rather turns what this king and his fate have come to symbolize into a celebratory cry of defiance. Using the words of a lauded (though importantly 'Queer') voice from the literary canon to communicate his meanings gives them added resonance – and, he suggests, got the piece funded. The 'dusty old play'[25] thus storms into the present, a mouthpiece for an angry activist.

This anger tells only half the story, however, for Jarman often uses his textual and filmic space for deeply personal reflection. In *Modern Nature*, for example, there is no linear drive to the conclusion of a narrative or argument and the text instead has its base in the tropic temporalities of the garden, gathering the folkloric associations of the plants, readings of the Dungeness landscape, memories and reflections into a personal mythology. 'The gardener', he writes, 'digs in another time, without past or future, beginning or end. A time that does not cleave the day with rush hours, lunch breaks, the last bus home'.[26]

There is a sense of literary and physical escape in *Modern Nature* and the garden it depicts. It is not a retreat into the past but into a re-affirming concurrent time where thoughts, associations and life itself are not subsumed by a domineering linear track. The John Donne poem ('The Sunne Rising') which Jarman printed on the wall of Prospect Cottage so that it overlooked the garden echoes the sentiment: the poet chides the sun and demands some space and time in which to love.

Similarly in *Chroma*[27] Jarman sets down a personal collection of associations, quotations, history and mythology around a number of colours. He employs Wittgenstein's style,[28] embodying thoughts or concepts in pithy epigrams which have only an oblique connection with those that come before and after, and could moreover gesture in any number of directions. The reader is drawn into (rather than past) each epigram and there is no concluding or objectifying drive which seeks to show what is written as universally 'true' or 'right': what he has collected are explicitly *his* thoughts and observations. The corollary is that we can do the same – by engaging us in each of his epigrams he implicitly endorses our departure from them to investigate our own set of associations. Jarman thus again sets out his perspective, but his 'I' is far from exclusive and he both embraces us in his vision and affirms the possibilities of difference beyond it.

The title of this essay – 'Words written without any stopping' – is the name of a poem in one of Jarman's first published works, *A Finger in the Fishes Mouth* (1972).[29] It characterizes his written work, particularly that of the early part of the 1990s, where his anger, thoughts, hopes and desires are set down with a sense of urgency. The collection itself almost completely lacks punctuation: one line flows into the next, and each poem gestures forward to the ones that follow, where thoughts and themes are re-explored from a different place and perspective – presaging his later work. There is a further thematic thread running through these poems, though, which testifies to the impossibility of ever comprehensively capturing experience and (a) life in the written word. The final elegiac poem ('Poem VII Farewell') ends:

> now in these our letters
> we are building a marble monument
> to cover a grave
> the days are numbered
> we have proven our loss

Writing indicates the loss of an 'original' and we can only ever chase it, attempt to tie it down. However much Jarman wrote it could clearly never properly capture him, but his commitment to writing – to continuing the chase – has left us with an impressive attempt. Jarman's final invitation is to take what he has produced, to use it, but again to move forward. In *At Your Own Risk* he gestures beyond the end of the text and his own life towards our future and possibilities. Thus the darkness in which he writes on Hampstead Heath at the start ('I don't know how long I spent there. My mind was racing. I was writing in the dark, angrily') finally opens out:

But as I leave you Queer lads let me leave you singing. I had to write of a sad time as a witness – not to cloud your smiles – please read the cares of the world I have locked in these pages; and after, put this book aside and love. May you of a better future, love without a care and remember we loved too. As the shadows closed in, the stars came out.
I am in love.[30]

Unless otherwise stated, all titles refer to works by Derek Jarman.
1 *A Finger in the Fishes Mouth*, Bettiscombe, Bettiscombe Press, 1972, poem 28.
2 *At Your Own Risk*, London, Vintage, 1993, p. 30.
3 *Dancing Ledge*, London: Quartet Books, 1991, p. 7.
4 *Ibid.*
5 *Dancing Ledge*, p. 60.
6 *Modern Nature*, p. 195.
7 *At Your Own Risk*, p. 41.
8 *Dancing Ledge*, p. 129.
9 *At Your Own Risk*, p. 5.
10 *Modern Nature*, London: Vintage, 1992, p. 69.
11 Blazdell, J., *Aids and the Borders of Postmodernity: from discriminating bodies to disseminating information*, PhD. thesis, University of London, 1994, p. 108.
12 Jarman in the BBC *Arena* documentary *Derek Jarman: a portrait* (1991).
13 *Queer Edward II*, London: BFI, 1991, p. 86.
14 *Queer Edward II*, p. 112.
15 *At Your Own Risk*, p. 47.
16 *The Last of England*, London: Constable and Co., 1987, p. 166.
17 Jarman in the BBC *Arena* documentary.
18 *Modern Nature*, p. 51.
19 *At Your Own Risk*, p. 20.
20 *At Your Own Risk*, p. 104.
21 *At Your Own Risk*, p. 111.
22 *Dancing Ledge*, p. 30.
23 *Caravaggio*, London: Thames and Hudson, 1986, p. 132.
24 *At Your Own Risk*, p. 46.
25 *Queer Edward II*, prologue.
26 *Modern Nature*, p. 30.
27 *Chroma*, London: Century, 1994.
28 See, for example, Wittgenstein, L., *Remarks on Colour*, ed. Anscombe, Oxford: Blackwell, 1979.
29 'Notes found on the body of a BA general student' was published prior to this in *Lucifer: Kings College Review*, Lent term, 1963.
30 *At Your Own Risk*, p. 134.

Borrowed Time

Stuart Morgan, lecturer in Contemporary Art History, the Ruskin School of Art

'I live on borrowed time. Therefore I see no reason in the world why my heart grows not dark. A cold wind blows tonight over this desolate island.' [1]

There is a Victorian *genre* which literary historians call the 'state of England' novel. In many ways, Derek Jarman's work occupies a similar category for our own time, more than a century later. But Jarman's response to his country seems paradoxical. For as a patriot who more than once described himself as a 'conservative'[2] and who felt free to celebrate the beauty and culture of Britain – 'English nostalgia is his danger', wrote one of his first reviewers[3] – Jarman nevertheless continued to rail against the hypocrisy of his countrymen and their failure of vision. His high opinion of his homeland and his disappointment in its shortcomings never changed. Shortly before Jarman death, he mounted a full-scale attack on the British gutter press and the mentality of its writers and readers: seeking informed, open-minded and creative people, he could find only paid representatives of a moral majority he despised.

In artworks made towards the end of his life he was attempting two things. First, to alert his viewers to the lies and bigotry purveyed by British newspapers and to the double standards of journalists and editors, and second to return to his first love: painting. By this time he was collaborating with the Pet Shop Boys, whom one might call a 'state of England' band, and tracing his own lineage to a collection of scapegoats or oddballs: in cinema to European masters such as Pier Paolo Pasolini, and in art to William Blake and Eric Gill, both persecuted British visionaries and free thinkers whose politics permeated their work as well as their lives. The 1960s, the period dearest to Jarman, were over – for indeed, by this time all that they stood for had been ruthlessly, almost systematically destroyed – and he needed to vent his anger and disgust with the values of subsequent decades. It was time for him to paint again. Painting, after all, was a uniquely personal medium; he would take his leave as he began. But this time he knew more. This time his mood would be Artaudian: it would take the form of a scream of rage, an attack on the gutter press and the moral low ground that British culture now occupied.

When they were made in London in 1992, the 'Queer' canvases seemed as out of joint as the times themselves, and perilously similar to pastiches of Abstract Expressionism, the *lingua franca* of Jarman's art-school years. In particular, they were close to the image that the American 1950s photographer Hans Namuth presented of Jackson Pollock as a potent, male hero and an outstanding participant in an exciting new movement. But the excitement was partly artificial, and the speed of the making and the fury of Pollock's paint application were fictions created by the camera. In fact the process of completing paintings was as lengthy as it was tiresome, punctuated by long breaks during which, with help from his wife, the painter Lee Krasner, he would lift the heavy, paint-laden canvases and fix them on the wall, a tediously slow undertaking. Namuth's camera showed only what appeared to be sudden outbreaks of physical violence, as if the process consisted of volcanic eruptions of genius and nothing more.

But if Pollock's *Sturm und Drang* was a figment of his publicists, Jarman's was certainly not. Could it be that in his last paintings he was symbolically making a will by deciding to act out its rituals for what he must have realised would be the last time? There were other differences too. Pollock's famous remark about 'veiling' his image[4] was exactly the opposite of Jarman's method in these late works; instead, Jarman pretended to uncover an existing image in the manner of an archaeologist. His viewers would watch it appear, then be abandoned. Once freed, it would be defaced by graffiti as posters are, as if theirs was an impermanent form of street life with sinister undertones. And indeed, the project proposed was one of investigation, from the depths of the unconscious mind. Possibly that is what Jarman thought he had suggested. But it is not what had happened at all.

In *Modern Nature*, Jarman uses the phrase 'wandering aimlessly in this labyrinth of memories', a good description of the unmethodical style of his own diaries, letting the mind ramble through past and present, noting pressures and counter-pressures at different times. That warring forces can also describe the structures of artworks becomes evident later in the same book, when an entry for one Sunday in January 1990 begins with the image of clouds obscuring the sun, then gives an account of the wind 'roaring across Gesualdo's madrigals', which Jarman characterizes as 'strange products of a Counter-Reformation psychosis working through a late medieval art form'. A note of perversity is sounded here. (Gesualdo is famous not only for his music but for his violence.) He implies that a sense of order in art can be polarized, and though the pressures might be irreconcilable, that a third, higher, hybrid organizational method may be produced. Presumably the secret was not to lose the melodic thread.

Jarman wrote in the script for *Jubilee*, 'You have to rely on your own immediate perception of the legitimate order.' In his last paintings, Jarman seems to acknowledge this order by wrenching it out of shape, pitting against each other different ways of organizing his material, as well as variations of rhythm and facture. So photocopies would be employed to offset thick, worked paint, hiding or revealing each other by turns. And words would be finger-painted, so that they were not only superimposed on the thick surface but would also become part of that surface, readable for their sense while simultaneously encouraging an abstract interpretation. Most importantly, different routes would be negotiated through the paintings but the relationships between those routes would vary, as would relationships between the readability of the words, perceptible only in patches and distracting one's attention from larger rhythms. The result would be a confrontation with surfaces which resembled painting but which instead were engaged on a double errand, offsetting one type of communication with another, matching one mode of reading – word for word – with what might be considered its polar extreme, interpretation.

Do Jarman's hand-painted words rise up from the paint or are they superimposed on it? It is hard to decide, given the width and height of each work and the background of repetitive newsprint, sometimes almost completely submerged in pigment. Jarman frequently painted into, not simply onto surfaces, as in *Toxo*, *Sick* and *EIIR*, a method which might have been inspired by the giant lead books of the German artist Anselm Kiefer, another painter with whom he had immediately felt an affinity. The result is difficulty in 'reading' the image. (Indeed, *Toxo* is short for toxoplasmosis, an infection which Jarman contracted, one result of which is loss of sight.) But the tangled quality of the information provided is also hard to construe.

In Jarman's paintings then, the visual field becomes a complex, densely worked site of simultaneous overlay and excavation. Kiefer's sense of history is undoubtedly present. Only one other influence looms larger: that of Pollock, not only because of the similarity of his and Jarman's painting but also because of the resonance of the message both men conveyed. His colleague Barnett Newman said: 'Pollock was more than a great "picture-maker": his work was *his* lofty statement in the grand dialogue of human passion, rich with sensitivity and sensibility. But it must not be forgotten that moving through the work is that revolutionary core that gave it life'.[5] A similar revolutionary fervour is present in Jarman, as if every mark he made was there to change your life. Although in one sense his art is more specific, more local than that of the great American masters of the 1950s, it recalls classic Abstract Expressionism nonetheless, if only because of the greatness of his theme: an issue of human rights involving a higher number of people than we could imagine.

Jarman was certainly revolutionary in his determination to attack Thatcherite callousness and the lingering damage done by the new Right: in particular their deliberate attempt to widen the social divide between 'haves' and 'have-nots', a particular instance of which, he insisted, was the reporting of AIDS, a mixture of scaremongering and (perhaps deliberate) obtuseness. Of course, patronizing writing in the press is based on a calculated decision not to try to educate your readership. In the case of AIDS awareness, however, the result could be accurately described as being contrary to the public good.

The 'Queer' paintings show printed paper fixed to a large canvas — photocopied headlines from front pages of tabloid newspapers, for example. These are then partly obscured, while at the same time making an underlying grid. This is one basic strategy of Modernism, both early and late, which serves to equalize the impact of each part of the canvas and to imbue the painting with a sense of airiness and freedom. The repeated words, like repeated Warhol portraits, lighten the effect, in turn serving to lessen the impact of each separate element instead of exaggerating it, so that a sense of release from choice, decision-making or focus is achieved; a parallel to the British population as treated by newspaper editors with purposely little grasp of issues, facts or fairness, men who ensure that their employees continue to patronize to readers day in, day out, in a format style with predictable portions of smut, stupidity and sheer bigotry. Their control forms an equivalent to brainwashing.

As a rule, Jarman's use of paint counteracts this; as an agent of destruction, veiling or sometimes obscuring the grid, which we sometimes recognize, sometimes only sense. The grid itself acts as a device for the eye but also as a kind of screen. His attack on this repressive 'brick wall' of negative propaganda was purposely cathartic, Expressionist in its conviction that emotion can be 'purged'.

In Greek tragedy, the shared release of grief or anger lay at the heart of the entire undertaking, a communal experience involving an audience (the population of a city), masked actors and a chorus which served to mediate between viewers and actors, making the audience aware of trials in their own lives: not singly, but as members of a society, each bound by the same laws and the same religion. The release of emotion that resulted was positive; it brought people together, gave them a feeling of unity as Greeks and made them better citizens. When Antigone, for example, defies the tyrant Creon, she also demonstrates the citizen's right to protest.

When Jarman made his last paintings, the performative aspects of painting had been brought to the fore as a protest against the 'brickwall' of propaganda against AIDS, and therefore against human rights. The ground that had been won in the 1960s was in danger of being lost, and the weapon with which newspapers were seeking to control their increasingly insensitive and uneducated readers was to play to their bigotry, in particular to their fear of homosexuals. In other words, Jarman had intervened in a power struggle, using his own status as an artist and film-maker in order to perform in public for what he knew would be the last time. The performative aspect which was lacking in Pollock, despite being attributed to him, was let loose on the canvases which towered over the sick Jarman, who painted standing on a ladder. His hero was Goya, he had always insisted, and Goya's deep, Spanish blacks haunt these late works: black for death, but not for extinction, for in Jarman's painting it is a rich repository which includes all the other colours. And alongside those blacks, the deep reds. Tragedy lies at the heart of Spanish culture, in the colours of the costume of the matador, and the daring of his ceremonial brush with death.

By the time Jarman made the 'Queer' paintings he was a dying man. He worked on them in Richard Salmon's studio in London, standing on a ladder, sometimes talking, but more often simply listening to music. But because he tired easily, now and again he would feel the need to climb down and lie, or even fall asleep, on the wooden floor until he was able to summon strength to continue. (Later, when making the 'Evil Queen' paintings, his last, he directed assistants who worked under his instruction.) Not surprisingly, his anger had intensified. Now a particular mixture of hatred, desperation and militancy was summoned up and the most insistent of the running references was to the street, the origin of all political change. Meditative, autobiographical, hilarious, agit-prop – an improbable combination, indeed – these works may have been created to remind both us and him of what he had achieved and of his continuing dedication to a cause.

Possibly the most striking feature of the last paintings was their uniformity. Most of them employ square stretchers, each 84 by 84 inches: a space tall enough to contain a person of normal height, with room to spare. Despite their abstractness, therefore, there is a nagging reminder of a person standing, arms outstretched, like the Vitruvian man of the Renaissance. Whether the works were planned or not, Jarman certainly managed to create the impression of total spontaneity, with one exception: the words or motifs, the least spontaneous features of the entire venture, had to be made last, like a signature. Words on paintings take two forms: either the writing is meant to vie or contrast with the other, non-referential language employed, or the two blend easily, as components of a single project. Here the overriding emphasis was on abstract values. Two paintings in particular, *Germs* and *Topsy-Turvy*, must have reminded Jarman of other, earlier images of revolution. Part of the script for *Jubilee*, Jarman's punk 'state of England' film, reads:

> A hand spins a blue globe, blotched with a
> black cancer, written on the carefully deleted
> countries are sinister messages.
> NEGATIVE WORLD STATUS
> NO REASON FOR EXISTENCE
> OBSOLETE[6]

Blotched, black, cancerous, England was negative indeed, and the messages were sinister in the extreme. The presence of a disease which challenged so much that was important to Jarman's existence had signalled the beginning of the end: a painful coda to a full and happy life.

One difficulty of dealing with AIDS, still a relatively little known condition and one that counters attempts to defeat it, is actually to describe it. So vexatious is the permanent state of misunderstanding that the two abstract paintings of the series come as a relief: unashamedly decorative, lightly drawn marks on the surface. Decoration is there to provide pleasure for the eyes; its very presence gives comfort. Yet ironically, it is the visible transformation of the skin surface which may have inspired *Germs* and *Infection*. Different in tone from the others in the series, they are nevertheless vital to the conception of the whole, like a reminder of a regular beat in music or dance, suggesting the breath of the body itself. Here the speed of the making of the marks is unimportant in comparison to the rhythms they establish. Only regular marks can provide the sense of life that is fundamental to art, music or dance in any culture, anywhere, at any time.

These two decorative paintings – possibly abstractions of sores – set the tone for the entire series, whose titles suggest a collection of black jokes – sometimes literally so. 'Germs' and 'topsy-turvy' sound like fanciful descriptions of the outward symptoms of AIDS, given by a bemused bystander, knowing something was wrong, perhaps, but behaving as if all would be for the best. The words suggest someone incapable of facing reality, who realizes the seriousness of the predicament but is afraid to name or confront it.

The titles for the other paintings in the series are all too knowing. The humour is abrasive, deliberately shocking by touching on taboo subjects: encroaching blindness (*Fuck Me Blind*), madness (*Do Lalley*), black humour (*Dead Sexy*), and jokes about burning in Hell (this, surely, is the joke which underlies

Bubble and Squeak) Others are simply about the need to cause trouble, irrespective of his audience or of canons of good taste. One painting, *Sightless*, was made after Jarman had been blind for several months. He painted the process of going blind by taking colour photographs of his retina and splattering them with paint, symbolizing those dots and splotches which had begun by interfering with his sight and which, by the end of his life, had totally obscured it.

The wish to forge some close link between his mortality and his art was a longstanding one. 'I'll be cremated,' he wrote, 'And have Christopher mix the ashes with black paint and paint five canvases which I'll have signed.' (Towards the end of his life, Andy Warhol, whom Jarman admired, stood behind a plate-glass window for hours in a New York nightclub, allowing fans to look at him, a play on ideas of intimacy or supposed intimacy.) 'It'll be my last artwork', Jarman added. 'It seems a sensible way to deal with it, to become a work of art and retain some value in death.'[7]

Perhaps the most disturbing aspect of these paintings is their incongruity. Despite the proximity to death, a frantic party atmosphere is conjured up, created with flamboyant hand movements and, at the end, words written over and through the thick impasto, using a phrase either invented beforehand or coined to accompany the mood created by the paint. Inscribed in black over a complex ground built up from yellow and red with splashes of blue and olive green, *Arse-Injected Death Syndrome* resembles a joke about homosexuality made by a queer-basher who is threatened yet attracted by the idea of anal sex. Built up with an unabashed sense of physicality, this painting shares some of the luscious colour sense of another 1950s American master, Willem de Kooning. Like finger painting, the red trails testify to joyous physical involvement on the part of a painter accustomed to paying close attention to the limits of the frame. Moreover, as in finger painting, the impression – hardly surprisingly – is one of joy in freedom, the kind of freedom good friends can celebrate. Hence the breaking of taboos in those titles; in *Fuck Me Blind*, the wild manneristic effect resembles the writing on a Gerald Scarfe cartoon, while *Scream* (recalling Edvard Munch's famous Expressionist painting) reminds us what 'queens' are supposed to do. Such levity may be the result of hysterics. But that hardly matters; screams of pain and screams of joy are often indistinguishable, after all. The situation of the hysterical figure on a bridge in Munch's painting is crucial to Jarman's revision of the Scandinavian masterpiece. At a mid-point, between two shores, the figure is seized by sudden panic. The resulting yell – all the more poignant for being silent – is an expression of some general, overwhelming crisis rather than a complaint about a single issue. Jarman's situation, over which

Scream, oil on canvas, June 1993

he had been losing control, was being forced upon him more pressingly as the weeks passed. As his life ebbed away, the coincidence between his own physical state and that of the world outside had never been closer.

1 Jarman, *Modern Nature*, London 1991.
2 *Modern Nature.*
3 Nigel Gosling *Observer Review*, 24 September 1967.
4 'Once when I asked Jackson why he didn't stop the painting when a given image is exposed, he said "I choose to veil the image".' Lee Krasner Pollock in interview with B. H. Friedman, in William S. Lieberman's introduction to *Jackson Pollock: Black and White* (exhibition catalogue), Marlborough-Gerson Gallery, New York, 1969.
5 Barnett Newman 'Jackson Pollock: An Artists' Symposium 1967' in Clifford Ross (ed.), *Abstract Expressionism: Creators and Critics* New York 1990, p. 147.
6 Derek Jarman *At Your Own Risk: A Saint's Testament*, London 1993, p. 118.
7 Jon Savage *England's Dreaming* 1992, p. 375. ('The World's End', scene 4 of *Jubilee*, 1977).

Silence
Mixed media, 1986

The Mistake, mixed media, December 1987
These Thoughts, mixed media, 1988

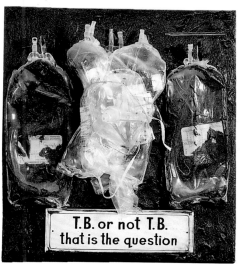

Prospect – The Shadow Takes on Substance, mixed media, 1987
TB or Not TB, mixed media, 1990

Landscape
Oil on canvas, June 1992

OPPOSITE
Above: *Landscape*
Oil on canvas, October 1991
Below: *Landscape*
Oil on canvas, 1991

COPIES SENT TO THE ARTS MINISTER

DEAR WILLIAM SHAKESPEARE
I AM 14 YEARS OLD AND I'M
QUEER LIKE YOU IM LEARNING
ART I WANT TO BE A QUEER ARTIST
LIKE LEONARD DI OR MICHELANGELO
BUT I LIKE FRANCIS BACON BEST
I READ ALLEN GINSBER RIMBAUD
I LOVE FILMS
I WILL MAKE THEM LIKE EISENSTEIN MURN
PASOLINI VISCONTI
DEREK

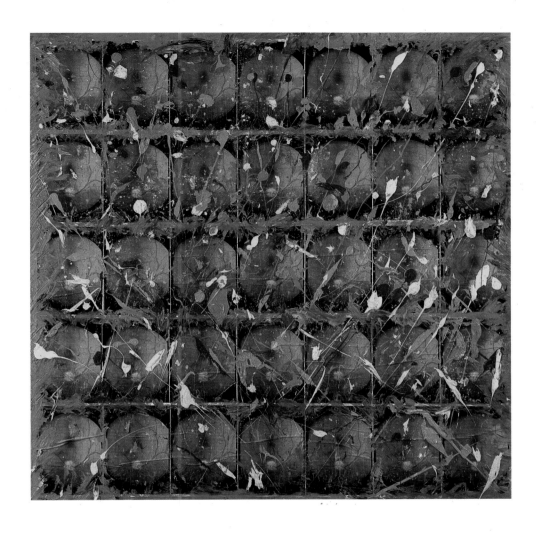

Sightless
Oil on colour photocopies on canvas, April 1993

OPPOSITE
Letter to the Minister
Oil on photocopies on canvas, 1992

Jarman at work on *Blood* in Richard Salmon's studio, 1992

OPPOSITE
Blood
Oil on photocopies on canvas, 1992

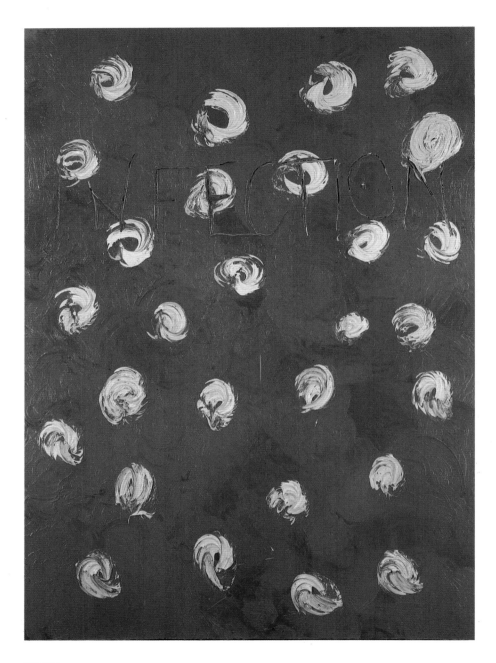

Infection
Oil on canvas, June 1993

Fuck Me Blind
Oil on canvas, June 1993

Do Lalley
Oil on canvas, October 1993

OPPOSITE
Spread the Plague
Oil on photocopies on canvas, 1992

Dipsy Do (Sinister)
Oil on canvas, October 1993

Dizzy Bitch
Oil on canvas, October 1993

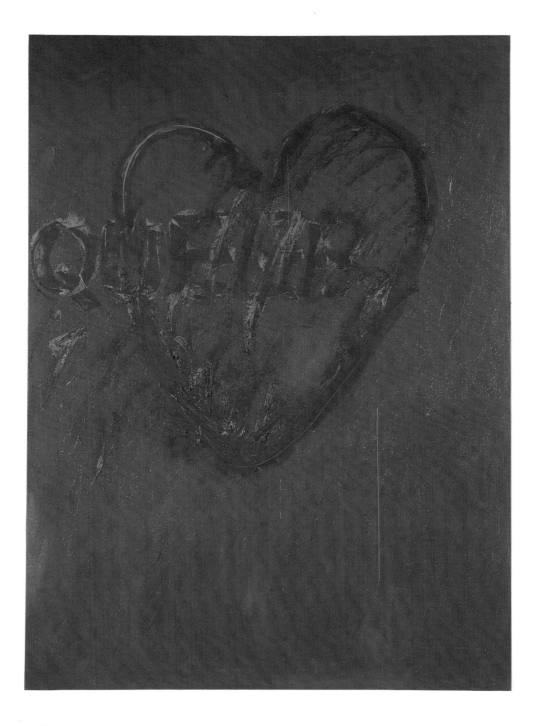

Et In Arcadia... Homo
Sexuality and the Gay Sensibility in the Art of Derek Jarman
James Cary Parkes, contributing editor, *Gay Times*

Plato says, as Montaigne reminds us in his essay *On the Cannibals*, that everything is contrived by Nature, Fortune and Art. In this scheme, Art is the lesser of the three elements – a bald imitation, an approximation, in a sense, a lesser expression of life. As an holistic theory of practice and form, Plato's order, perhaps, draws us close to Derek Jarman's work – in which the 'Ideal' might be expressed by degrees of incompletions and inexactitudes through Art, but only fully delineated by Nature and Fortune.

Jarman's art is informed by powerful desires, and a belief that aesthetics might provide useful allegories on life, express the passion of experience and qualify existence. His work both quantified and exemplified that experience of homosexuality left fallow and derided by an ever-hostile heterosexual society and its attendant artists. Romantic, *recherché* and absolutely raw, Jarman's vision was not of life lived through art but of art as an epigram of life. Always pointedly political, his work was employed as activism – a novel and lively debate in which the purpose was praxis, never quiet and veiled art-house reflection.

It is perhaps peculiar that in the 1980s and 1990s, for homosexuals a period of fierce anxiety and drive, the singular personification of gay rights should be an artist and not a politician; and that this artist should have such a sense of the quasi-mystical, the ethereal and the past. But for gay men the complexities of social pressure and political frustration no doubt require a political approach that fires the imagination, and one which is filled with compassion.

Politics in Jarman's work was never so simple as to be didactic. His activism was fuelled by ethical investigations. His morality was an old one – retold through fables and legends, and explored through the fierce anger of the editing table and in the frenetic application of oil, glass, tar and photocopies of tabloid newspaper cuttings onto canvas (pp. 121–9).

The spectre of haunted and desolate places runs through Jarman's art. From the ruined cityscapes of latter-day Elizabethan London (*Jubilee* and *The Last of England*), ancient Thebes (in the unrealized script of *Akhenaten*), the vanquished court of a medieval king (*Edward II*) to the unseen and uncertain streets of *Blue*. Jarman presents a picture of a world in which notions of physical decay and abandonment are inevitable, and inevitably befall the brave, but this discordant perspective is balanced by successively redemptive narratives.

Queer, oil on canvas, 1992

The spirit of a soul – the heretic Pharaoh Akhenaten, the apocalyptic heroes of *Jubilee*, the lovers of *The Last of England* – survives. And in this we witness a constant struggle – a form of collective pull, which if we were to describe it in terms of religious metaphor, is one of transfiguration: a blaze of optimism and eventual endurance.

1: Nature and Death

All was foretold me; naught
  Could I foresee;
But I learned how the wind would sound
  After these things should be.
Edward Thomas, THE NEW HOUSE

In order to understand the significance of Jarman's importance to gay culture, especially in the its context of the AIDS epidemic, his notion of death and its repetitive intrusion into his art is important. For within this are signals to the form Jarman saw in life and all activity. In this system of sometimes bitter deathly iconography, *endings* are, paradoxically, invariably eluded. Involved with this is a perhaps somewhat arcane notion of nature itself – a scheme that lent increasing value and purpose to Jarman's work as his life moved into the time of AIDS and his own, eventual death from the violence of an invisible virus.

Even before AIDS, gay art and the 'homosexual sensibility' wore the weight of elegy. Melancholy and mourning are the poetic legacies of prosaic oppression and menace – this is not to say that the tradition of *outsider* existence is necessarily tragic or dour, but rather that a history of brutal and ethically unjust treatment endows a particular perspective on society. This history finds an expression in Jarman's art which both celebrates gay love but is also antagonistic, introspective and sensitive to the fragility of order, law and the wider society in which that love exerts its existence. Like the Arcadian shepherds depicted in Poussin's paintings discovering the legend *Et in Arcadia Ego*, Jarman was drawn to remind us in his art that even in the most unexpected places, Death (in its many guises) intrudes. For gay men this is an objectively political message as well as a culturally explored expression. Jarman's films, writings and paintings are replete with metaphors for the transgression of danger into all activity, however innocent or 'natural'.

'I collected together the few landscapes that I painted with varnish glazes, pencil and metal dust.... Apocalyptic visions of fire, with skulls and minute people lost in eternity under strange moons' wrote Jarman in *Dancing Ledge* (1991, p. 222), describing paintings he put together for an exhibition in 1981. It was that year in which the AIDS virus was first detected amongst the cosmopolitan gay communities of New York and California. Still unseen in the United Kingdom, AIDS was to pervade European gay culture a few years later. And yet, at the unperceived inception of the epidemic, Jarman utilized the phraseology and obsessions which were to push into the forefront of gay culture during the mid-1980s and beyond. Nature and the landscapes that men made within it always contained a sinister and unsettling subtext. Jarman's aesthetic language was essentially one that disputed, and yet was excited by, a world in which comfort and stability were mercurial and suspect. If he employed the language of the Romantics before the onset of AIDS, then with the presence of the epidemic, his vision became one akin to the Georgian poets, when a metabolic war made that foreboding he had felt before a reality.

With this virus (and his own HIV-positive diagnosis in 1986) Jarman expanded his repertoire of metaphors. Beginning to make his now famous garden at Dungeness, Jarman acknowledged and worked within the fragility of temporality and corporeality. From the film *War Requiem*, by way of the Dungeness garden, to the making of his last 'Queer' paintings, Jarman created a vision that explored notions of loss, pain, resilience and struggle. These, in total, reflect the preoccupations of the gay community especially during the 1980s and 1990s. Activism in the guise of art, they philosophically complemented the emerging politics of ACT UP, Queer Nation and OutRage!. Indeed, as the 1980s merged into the 1990s, the jargon and flair of neo-queer politics and polemic found places (just as punk had during the 1970s) in Jarman's art and writing. Probably the most outré expression of this was to be the startling sight of modern gay activists rushing into a scene of the film *Edward II* to do battle with various bishops and nobles who were poised to kill the hapless homosexual monarch.

But this propensity to see the world in terms of its dangers, dilemmas and proximity to death was nothing novel in Jarman's art – it was prefigured in the insecurities and trepidation always current within the gay experience.

The image of the homosexual as martyr is a familiar motif. Desire and repression, castigation and destruction are elements that at once conform to the image of gay men as victims and yet fuel gay indignation and anger. It is in this latter sense that Jarman utilized impressions of loss and death so successfully in his art. From the slaying of St Sebastiane to the murder of King Edward II, the morbid alienation of Wittgenstein to the almost casual killing of Caravaggio,

Jarman sought out images of persecution, with which, in turn, he drew savage indictments of a relentlessly cruel and bitter world. Such perspectives gave rise to rallying calls for gay rights and a justification of queer history.

Amid these pictures of mortality stripped of melancholia was a force of wit and farce. 'Dear God, send me to hell' was a legend to be found inscribed in one of his paintings. Jarman's resistance to contemporary moral values employed an especially virile form of wit and irony and was both a symptom of the injustice he perceived around him and an ambitious swipe of self-defence.

As an iconoclast with an almost evangelical cause, Jarman rummaged through the arcane ruins of an ever-romantic England with the expectant hope that desire and love could be retrieved even from the trashed traditions of classical learning, art and literature. Searching through Jarman's art and films, including much made before the time of AIDS, we find sketch after sketch in which death and torture play upon the imagination. And these are no mere sadomasochistic indulgences – they show a passionate pathos to be found elsewhere in English art, from the poems of Shelley to the paintings of Francis Bacon. They are a pathology of pain; a portrait of the homosexual experience. Put to more pointed use during the AIDS epidemic, Jarman's work brilliantly illuminates strategies of resistance – the emotional and physical encumbrance of gay men at battle with not only the 'body politic' but also with the body itself.

2: Sex and Sexuality

But we, while we are intent upon one object,
already feel the pull of another. Conflict
is second nature to us. Aren't lovers
always arriving at each others boundaries? –
although they promised vastness, hunting, home.
Rainer Maria Rilke, THE FOURTH ELEGY

'The degree and kind of a person's sexuality reaches up into the topmost summit of his spirit,' wrote Nietzsche in his *Psychological Observations*, no doubt to the incomprehension of many readers both in the nineteenth century and today.

Homosexuality and its practise are inextricable from Jarman's art. From the sparsely detailed paintings of his adolescence, from which we decipher the loneliness and unrequited longing of gay youth, through to the energetic exuberance of sexual maturity and subcultural community throughout the 1970s and 1980s, Jarman's sexuality is the keystone of his artistic commitment.

Jarman's films, fine art and writings map the evolution of gay sexuality, both as a collective sentience and individual experience. Pre-Liberation (1960s), Post-Liberation (1970s) and the period of AIDS (1980–) are well documented in his art: the introspective and coded symbolism of his early work which revolves around his study at King's College London and the Slade; the frantic, intricately choreographed orgies which find their focus in the dance before the Emperor Diocletian in the prologue of the film *Sebastiane*, expressing the zeal and display of 1970s gay sexuality; the unsettling sexual scenarios of Jarman's 1980s films, (for example the symbolic rape of Caravaggio's *Profane Love* in *The Last of England*), which express the pessimism and disquiet of the Thatcher era and the moral panic emerging in response to HIV and AIDS; and into the 1990s with his elegant, nostalgic and rather sad observations on desire and sex-as-memory.

Jarman viewed his sexuality through the progress of four decades – each different in tone and timbre from each other. In fact, his career, both professional and 'sexual', runs in concert with the modern gay experience. Thus, in many ways, his work forms an ongoing commentary on the twists and shifts of *his* community. And with this comes a certain contradiction in expressions of sex and sexuality. From the affirmative and quite brash practices of the 1970s, the bruised and yet still kicking outrage of the 1980s, to the often sentimental though determined and resistant gay maturity of the 1990s, Jarman was an almost unique story-teller of gay desire.

It was to the Seventh Level of Hell that Dante dispatched homosexuals, just as a myriad of pre-medieval, medieval and modern thinkers cast down sodomites, inverts, homosexuals, queers and gays...

It was against an accumulated heritage of homophobic terror that Jarman played his part – knowingly and audaciously. Taking apart history, especially in his films, Jarman rooted out the discrepancies of acquired learning. A subversive academic, he mocked, mauled and made use of the past. A process of invention and

Jarman prior to publication of *At Your Own Risk*, 1992

The Canonization of St Derek, 22 September 1991

reclamation is both necessary and inevitable for any cultural exponent of a subjugated group, class or race. Gay historians, theorists and artists are driven to make of us a fragmented history. Jarman did this with relish and ease. His work is filled with artefacts brought from a forgotten past to the present in order to legitimize and ornament contemporary gay culture. And in this is an act of pure politics, albeit one that adhered to the ethics of personal identity and struggle.

Sex acts and sexuality were the objects of Jarman's archaeological sorties into the literature of the past. From Shakespeare's homo-erotic sonnets (*The Angelic Conversation*) to the crown of a king (*Edward II*), relics and rhetoric were re-appropriated. A totally queer conceit, indeed.

The historian Jeffrey Weeks has written, 'Sexuality could be a potentiality for choice, change and diversity' (*Sexuality and its Discontents*, 1985); this Jarman embraced with formidable gusto. Although much of his work appears to consider time as an ahistorical concept, in which a romantic and universal exploration of sexual practice was undertaken, these were in fact rather poetic lendings with which he drew analogies to examine very modern dilemmas at the core of theoretical and political issues: of sexual plurality, civil and human rights and a less tangible, though nevertheless passionately felt, desire for *a better world*.

Homosexuality, in Jarman's art, is often pictured in a state of siege and entrenchment. Ironically, homosexual practices themselves recur as methods of cruelty and torture employed against gays. The deaths of Edward II, St Sebastiane, the violence of the militia in *The Last of England* and the inverted tabloid vocabulary figuring in many of his fine art works speak not of self-hatred or masochistic propensities but of hypocrisy and absolute terror. They also function as a parody of authority; partially camp, strikingly confrontational, such scenarios re-employ the language of gay love to combat homophobia.

Unfettered desire and love is, however, to be found in Jarman's oeuvre. Perhaps the most spectacular, tender and expressive portrait of gay love is *The Angelic Conversation* (1985). In slow-time, inter-cut with dazzling, blanched montages, *The Angelic Conversation* converts the multi-interpretative love sonnets of William Shakespeare into outré protestations of gay desire. A visual blur of light and shade, of contracted and expanded time-scales, the film has the quality of dream-making. But even here the spectre of loss intrudes as the sonnets muse on death and passing; expressions abound of perfect moments intercut with a harsher reality. In one sense, *The Angelic Conversation* expresses much that Jarman personally felt about gay love, of its context and its contours, and marks an end to his quiet and relatively tranquil meditations on romance. The late 1980s and early 1990s saw much more pointed work, both in his cinema and painting. AIDS and moral panic made their marks as Jarman perceived gay culture to be at a crucial point of crisis. His response to AIDS culminated in the moving film *Blue* and his answer to homophobic hysteria ended with his final 'Evil Queen' paintings made shortly before his death.

3: Activism and Art

If you're not angry then you can't be fighting very hard.
Derek Jarman in an unpublished interview, 1992

Gay politics and notions of a Gay Community are ever-changing affairs. Reactive to the times in which they are placed, the politics of homosexuality (and its *aesthetic* expression) and the concept of a Gay Community do have tangible points in common from decade to decade. Familiar, generational connections are to be found. And it is these that Jarman drew upon; he talked of the past to reinforce and colour the urgency of present struggles and place them in a continuum of defiance and battle.

To ask what activism is in a gay context we must be aware that the very existence (let alone the *activity*) of homosexuality is taken in hostile quarters as a state of rebellion, decadence and crime. Thus, in one scheme of thought at least, all action has a political nature and all open displays are some form of activism. In the 1970s Jarman's contribution to gay politics was, in part, his revelry in the public expression of what had hitherto been both private and indeed illegal. A sly glimpse of an erection (*Sebastiane*), the assimilation of stable gay couples within the context of anarchic and entirely dysfunctional heterosexual relationships (*Jubilee*) as well as the serious frivolity (sic) of his involvement with Andrew Logan's *Alternative Miss World* (p. 165) all express a value in exposing in an undisguised or relatively uncoded fashion homosexuality both as a celebration and as a form of agitation for acceptance and change.

In the 1980s Jarman's activism retained its personal edge but was nevertheless focused into what might be better understood as rhetoric and polemic. Amongst the first to perceive the period as one of heightened reaction and repression, Jarman was fiercely involved in debates about the censorship of art and homosexuality. In fact, *The Last of England* might be read as an indictment of Thatcherist practice, as a mourning for lost liberality and a foreboding of how the State was shaping the lives of all those falling from conventional norms.

Jarman eloquently wrote about his own HIV diagnosis, which he took as not only a metabolic occurrence but also as a metaphoric happening. An accident of biology stood as an illustration of how society actually was – a dangerous and inexorable place. Jarman did, however, remain consistent in his uncompromising attitude towards sexual politics. Just as he had created poetic work from physical intimacy in the 1970s, in the 1980s and 1990s he continued to enthuse about the strength of sexual contact. Even if Arcadia was blighted by the presence of Death, Hampstead Heath remained a place in which he found solace and inspiration. Even though his critics described the sexual interest which invariably flowed through his work as, at best, an echo of some lost Edenic world, Jarman saw only a harmonious link between the energy of sexuality in the 1960s and 1970s, and its urgency and necessity in the 1980s and 1990s.

Blue (1993) is a codicil of kinds in which he explores, without visual images, the experience of HIV and illness. 'The virus rages fierce. I have no friends now who are not dead or dying. Like a blue frost it caught them,' says Jarman's narrative. No doubt, reminiscent of the spirit of the *fin de siècle*, *Blue* is a homage to each part of his life touched upon in his earlier works: love, death, sexuality, tradition, romanticism. For gay men in the time of AIDS, however, *Blue* is a perfect synthesis of melancholy and memorial, of reflection and resilience.

For all the quiet elegance of *Blue,* the 'Queer' paintings represent Jarman's last great rally against homophobia. Immediately we are taken back to the power of *Jubilee*, the quantified rage of *The Last of England* and the confidence of *Caravaggio*. It was certainly fitting that Jarman chose painting to be almost his final act of art agitation; painting was after all his primary medium. The 'Queer'

Jarman at a demonstration outside the *Guardian* newspaper offices, 1991

series, which the critic Simon Watney has called 'tactless pictures, which draw attention to ugly emotions in order to refute them', are virulent, highly charged pieces. Taking headlines hostile to homosexuality and those with AIDS from the British tabloid press, Jarman drowned them with heavy oils and varnish (pp. 126–9). They are a peculiar and savage form of collage. Applied with great speed and gusto, the paint is both a response to the text and a statement beyond them. Confirming the greater issues of painting – Sex, Love and, of course, Death – they have tremendous aesthetic as well as polemical impact. What at first appears to be an act of pure iconoclasm turns into a finer and more useful homage to an idealism of difference. The ugliness of hysteria is worked away under brushstrokes and what is finally left is an impression of artistic and activist penetration of every avenue of resistance.

Blue and the 'Queer' paintings are a robust legacy. In them we see the force of idealism and a potent expression of artistic skill. The Derek Jarman canon examined the dilemmas and delight within the modern gay experience. Art's only relevance, his work shows, is in its proximity to life – as a way in which we *draw* ourselves. With a licence to communicate the extreme, the unsettling and to exaggerate the beautiful, Derek Jarman is the single most important gay artist of the Post-Liberation period.

The Jarman Garden Experience

Christopher Lloyd, gardening correspondent for *Country Life* and the *Guardian*

It was on 24 June 1990 that, quite accidentally, I happened on Derek Jarman's garden. Five of us – Beth Chatto being the picnic maker – plus my two dachshunds, spent this sunny day on the beach at Dungeness. The shingle drops steeply into deep sea and Channel traffic passes quite close by. No bathers – too dangerous for that, and there have been numerous shipwrecks here, where opposing currents meet. There are anglers and plenty else to watch. Robin constructed a little boat from bits of flotsam lying around, using a scrap of stiff plastic for a sail. He launched it and we watched it bobbing merrily about till it disappeared from sight in the direction of Hythe.

All the land behind us has been wrested from the sea, shingle piling on shingle – beach, it is known as, locally – a huge, ever-increasing promontory of it. Presently, a fishing boat came in and landed its catch a couple of hundred yards along the shore. Leaving the others to carry our things to my car and to drive it closer to the fishing boat along the road that runs parallel to the shore, Beth and I hastened to see what had been caught. Nothing exciting (no John Dory, which I had first seen here many years before). The men were grumpy, anyway; tired, most likely.

We walked towards the car and then I spotted some brilliant flower colour; I headed for it. Houses, well separated, are strung out along this road on its inland side. There are no visible boundaries or fences. I made a beeline for that colour. It hadn't just happened, like the wild flowers that make such vivid displays beneath the dazzling openness of the sky, yet nowhere else were any of the habitations making the slightest attempt to garden. Here, around a timber cottage tarred black but with cheerful yellow window frames, a garden had been made.

Most brilliant were the Californian poppies (eschscholzias), wide open to the sun. But so much else. 'Come over here, Beth', I called out and a moment later we were both excitedly examining the apparently deserted scene, myself taking photographs and scribbling a list of the plants so evidently happy here, in the back of my pocket diary.

Presently, from a neighbouring house, a young man came up behind me, as I crouched. 'I expect you want to know what we're doing', I said to him, 'I can see what you're doing', he replied. And he left us to it.

June is a good moment in this area. Gale-force winds have temporarily let up and there is a great burst of colour from wild flowers, many of which were included in this garden, either because they were already there or because they had been added. But although the vegetation of early summer had masked a good deal, there was evidence of design here, with arrangements, often in circles, of flints and other stones, sea-smoothed bricks, sea shells and more besides. Also of 'sculpture' with all kinds of legacies from the war, fishing accessories and sea defences.

We gradually worked our way around to the front of the house where two raised beds with a fair amount of soil in them were growing a different range of plants from those which the shingle could support. How surprised we were when the door opened and Derek Jarman stepped out. My young friends knew him at once and were star-struck. Being of an older generation and having long ceased to visit movies, I did not know him and he did not expect me to. But it was not long afterwards that I made a point of seeing his latest film, *The Garden*, in London, and I then realized what all the interest and excitement was about.

Jarman knew about Beth, through a friend; of her garden and nursery. Whether he had heard of me, I do not know, but he visited my nursery fairly frequently towards the end of his life and got to know my garden, which he mentioned very appreciatively in his own garden book. I came to Prospect Cottage again, two summers later, and met him once at my home, Great Dixter. He was frail and in a wheelchair. I had hoped to get him over to dinner, but that never happened.

His garden lies around the house, but mostly fore and aft in roughly equal proportions. The principal feature in a flat landscape is the Dungeness nuclear power station. It is not a romantic scene, being scattered with huts and sporadic habitations, with pylons and overhead cables and power lines. But is is open and it smells good. Mainly of the sea, of course, but also of flowers and plants in their season.

Sea kale (*Crambe maritima*) is the dominant plant, more abundant here than anywhere else in the British Isles. It is the first colonizer above the tideline, with tap roots that delve in search of moisture. Jarman quoted 20 feet as a root length, measured on a plant that had become exposed after a storm. If you were to plant sea kale, you would need to start with a section of root, and that would make shoots and its own roots. But I fancy the plants were all in place in this garden already; Jarman made them the centre of formal circles that he built.

Young sea kale shoots first become visible in March and the new foliage is purple, later becoming blue-grey. It is crinkly and cabbage-like, the flowers are gathered into large, white cumulus clouds that smell of honey on the air, the first to open, in early May, being those that are lying against the 'beach' and receive extra heat from sun-warmed stones. The flowers are followed by huge tangles of pea-sized fruits, which take months to ripen and eventually become 'the colour of bone. At this stage they are at their most beautiful – sprays of pale ochre, several thousand seeds on each plant' (*Derek Jarman's Garden*, p. 16).

Gorse (*Ulex europaeus*) is abundant on the Ness and sends the smell of coconut into the air. Rabbits graze gorse as high as they can reach, which makes it very dense. When flowering, the rabbit-grazed surfaces are solid with blossom. Jarman planted two circles of gorse, with a baulk of timber standing vertically in the centre of each. Blackthorn blossom (*Prunus psinosa*) is a great feature, all over the shingle in April, the bushes far lower than normal, often hugging the ground and flowering early as a consequence. Jarman waged war on the browntail moth caterpillars that wreak havoc in blackthorn foliage.

Broom, *Cytisus scoparius*, comes next, again reduced in height and making pools of yellow, of a brighter shade than gorse but sour-smelling. Other good scents, mainly from the garden, include santolina, the grey lavender cotton, planted in formal circles. To be kept neat, it needs clipping and this prevents flowering, which is an undistinguished event anyway. Then, *Helichrysum angustifolium*, the curry plant which smells strongly exactly of that. With narrow, grey leaves, it is used formally like the santolina, but is allowed to carry its huge crop of yellow flowers, being clipped over in August. 'Helichrysum, in which the lizards dance, is the backbone of the garden, both in the formal garden at the front and at the back', Jarman wrote.

Herbs are strongly featured. Jarman describes *Ruta graveolens* as turning 'into a tight rue football'. He probably gave that a hard, annual clip-back. Lavender is very much at home. Any plant with a hairy, grey-white leaf, or glaucous, with a wax-coated leaf (like sea kale and rue), is geared to coping with sun, wind and arid conditions at the root. Jarman was always a passionate gardener, from earliest childhood, and he well understood which plants would like him under these extreme conditions. On my heavy clay, lavender hates me, growing scraggily and frequently leaving me with gaps in lavender hedging. I have learned to live without it. Rosemary, closely related to lavender, thrives at Prospect Cottage, as do sage and marjoram. The shrubby, grey filigree-leaved old man, *Artemisia abrotanum*, with its curious, pungent smell is here, and also absinth, *A. absinthium*. Lovage and fennel have deep, fleshy roots and they are good. Borage grows here but its cousin, the biennial viper's bugloss (*Echium vulgare*), is one of the showiest natives. In its first year, it makes a starfish of ground-hugging foliage. In its second, it sends spikes of blue flowers up to 2 feet high. Imagine them combined, as here, with crimson field poppies, *Papaver rhoeas*. But Jarman also loved 'the sky blue cornflower which comes up in every corner'. That is an excellent poppy companion.

The wild, or introduced and feral, plants on the Ness are a significant feature. Some were already in this garden. Others Jarman introduced so as to have them in a concentration, which is what gardening is largely about. He did not have to bring them far. In my garden, I consider toadflax (*Linaria vulgaris*) a weed, not merely because it has a running, invasive rootstock, but because it grows in a straggling, weedy way. Not here. Colonizing, yes, but short and with a dense spike in two shades of yellow – a kind of mini-snapdragon with a spur at the back. We normally think of foxgloves as tall inhabitants of coppiced woodland. Here, they are equally happy but not much more than 2 feet high and with more intensely rose-purple flowers on an exceptionally dense spike.

The horned poppy, *Glaucium flavum*, has scalloped grey foliage in its first year, which alone would make it worth growing, but in its second makes a 2- to 3-foot branching inflorescence, producing a succession of fragile yellow poppy flowers, each lasting just one day. Valerian (*Centranthus ruber*), pink, red and white, grows near the road over many parts of the Ness. Jarman rightly observes that it will have a second flowering, particularly if cut back after the first flowering in June. 'I have always loved this plant. It clung to the old stone walls of the manor at Curry Mallet which my father rented in the early fifties, and grew in the garden of the bomb-damaged house at the end of the road which the airman Johnny, my first love, took me to on his motorbike, with my hands in his trouser pockets – so valerian is a sexy plant for me.'

Rest-harrow, *Ononis repens*, was a favourite and Jarman showed me where it was growing on the roadside hard by, better than in his own garden. It is a spiny, grey-leaved plant that makes a foot-tall mound and is covered with pale pink pea flowers. Normally, I associate it with chalk downland, but alkaline conditions prevail equally along our shores, where broken seashells abound.

Jarman grew not only *Rosa rugosa*, which is introduced but wonderful near the sea, and the dog rose, *R. canina*, but also the burnet rose, *R. pimpinellifolia*, a true wilding of shingle. Only a foot tall, under starvation conditions, it creeps around making a colony and opens its cream-coloured flowers as early as May.

Elder is one of the taller shrubs, here, but still not much above 6 feet high, as its wood is soft and anything with the temerity to put its head up must take a battering. I think it looks dreadful under such conditions, but Jarman loved it. He had four specimens, one at the front, three at the back. He valued them for the culinary uses that their flowers can be put to, quite rightly ignoring their fruits, which taste disgusting. But in respect of the shrub itself, he saw a beautiful shape 'made of a thousand small branches'. The fact that the plant kept its 'bone-coloured dead branches' made it look the more attractive, to him, as did the dead branches of dog roses, 'pink-grey, swaying in the wind'. This bleached, dead look strongly appealed to him, witness the abundance of driftwood that was brought in to ornament the garden.

Two large, loose shrubs, soft in texture and fast growing, that flourish by the sea are the pinky-mauve tree mallow, *Lavatera olbia*, and the so-called tree lupin, *Lupinus arboreus*, with pale yellow, sweetly scented spikes and fresh green foliage. It always surprises me that such soft shrubs, breaking up so easily when gale-force winds blow in inland gardens, yet should never be so happy as on the coast. The mallow flowered next to Derek Jarman's 'throne', hard up against the inland side of the house. Here, too, grew the exotic relative of seakale, *Crambe cordifolia*, which makes an 8-foot-high cloud of tiny white blossom. Much more exposed, the giant cardoon stands strong against all winds. Drawn up to 9 feet in my mixed border, it needs the stoutest staking. This is the wild version of globe artichoke, with smaller, more numerous heads and much more prickly.

I felt sorry for bearded irises, whose fragile blooms get torn immediately on opening, even in quite moderate winds – as winds go, hereabouts. Tougher stalwarts included yucca and phormium, the New Zealand flax, often planted as a first defence against the wind, along coastal shores.

Of smaller, ground-hugging plants, the silver cushions of pinks and carnations are in their element. And thrift, *Armeria maritima*, the sea pink of Scotland, but its cushions are green. Jarman actually bought his first plant of this but it soon became fifty and was poised to leap across the road. Because it did not come of its own volition, I suppose ecologists would disapprove. The sea campion, with inflated bladders behind white petals, is everywhere on the Ness and is in this garden. Two native stonecrops make pools of fleshy leaves, tight against the stones. *Sedum acre*, a dashing shade of yellow; *S. anglicum* with flesh pink stars. Gazanias hail from South Africa, but revel in conditions such as these, their daisies, in many shades and so beautifully marked, expanding to the warmth of sun and shingle. Seldom hardy, inland, their chances of being perennial would be more than doubled here.

Jarman did not leave matters to chance when seeking to establish new plants. To make a planting hole, the shingle had to be excavated and half of it would always roll back, so it was an effortful job. Then he put in well rotted manure from the farm up the road, and the stones were returned at the end of the operation. He told me that he dribbled the seeds of annuals into the cracks between stones. If one took off, thereafter it would ripen and disseminate its own seed. That was the way with eschscholzias, wallflowers, stocks and marigolds (*Calendula* not *Tagetes*).

There is a vegetable and herb garden. The bed was lined with black polythene, to keep in the moisture – this spot has the lowest rainfall in Britain – filled in with topsoil, delivered by dealer, and then well dunged. The vegetables and herbs protect the beehive. Pounds of honey were made, far more than Jarman wanted for himself, so some was given away and plenty left for the bees. Flowers on the Ness provide abundant nectar. The nearest rape, four miles distant, would be beyond the bees' normal foraging range.

The garden's layout and ornamentation make a very strong impression. The area between road and cottage, down which a straight driveway once led, now consists of a series of large circles outlined with stones which Jarman collected himself, a few at a time, arranged according to colour, the elongated ones on end. Flints can be large and long (high), and could form the circle's hub, though sea kale also makes the focus, in some instances. Shells and coloured stones from the beach make up the surface between circles of standing stones or dragon's teeth (pp. 154–5).

Any stones with holes in them have been collected and threaded into necklaces, which are hung in all sorts of places, or dropped over anything pointed, like the tines of a garden fork. Sculptures, which are mostly found objects, sometimes assembled, sometimes standing on their own, consist of anything that the area can produce, including the heads of old garden tools. On the morning of my second visit, a schoolgirl had brought a piece of twisted iron which she had found. The balls of metal floats are here and the corks which are another kind of float. Chains, anchors, a hook, wartime fence posts, with one end in a spiral for the threading of barbed wire, and much more besides. I never saw this scene in winter, when it must have looked stark, but in summer, all was softened by vegetation.

This was and still is a quite extraordinary garden. Derek Jarman made and retained devoted friends, who helped him increasingly as he became feebler. Good luck to them, in keeping Prospect Cottage and its garden going. They are besieged with visitors, swarming to this Mecca. Many of my own visitors make a point of going to have a look. Prospect Cottage is very much in the English garden tradition, showing a love of plants and growing them well as a personal satisfaction. Like all good gardeners, Jarman worked with the natural conditions presented to him by the locale. The fact that he was not put off by being told that gardening at Dungeness was 'impossible', and of there being no protocol or guidance, is also in the English tradition. I feel privileged to have been on the scene when I was, though sad that an acquaintanceship had not the time to become much more than that. Jarman was a man whom I regarded deeply and his garden was a manifestation of great depth and total originality.

World War II beach defence and driftwood,
with cotton lavender

FOLLOWING PAGES: Prospect Cottage,
Dungeness, summer 1992

Ego et in Arcadia
Oil on canvas with metal foil, 1992

OPPOSITE
Looking out to sea from the front door
of Prospect Cottage, summer 1991

FOLLOWING PAGES Jarman with his
head resting on a sea kale during the
filming of *The Garden*, 1990

Chronology

1942–67

1942 Derek Jarman was born at Northwood, Middlesex on 31 January, the son of Lancelot Elworthy Jarman, a serving RAF officer, who was born in New Zealand, and Elizabeth Evelyn (Betty) Jarman (neé Puttock), born in India, who studied at Harrow School of Art and worked for a time for the couturier Norman Hartnell.

1942–50 The Jarman family lived for varying lengths of time in England, Pakistan and Italy, before returning to England.
1946 Jarman's first known surviving artwork, a Christmas card.

1947–55 Between 1947 and 1950 Jarman attended three primary schools (including a Roman Catholic one) before starting at Hordle House School at Milford on Sea. He won prizes for his gardening and took part in school plays, acting the parts of Cruel Frederick in *Struwwelpeter* and the Aga of Nutty Slack in *Kidnabbed* by Bobby Loony Ravingsoon (aka Philip Howard, one of the staff). His 1948 report noted his drawing showed originality and his handiwork was very good.

1955 Attended Canford School in Dorset. He became increasingly active in the art hut, a retreat from other less agreeable aspects of public school life, where his artistic development was loosely guided by the art master, Robin Noscoe. He exhibited and sold work at Canford and designed the set for *Julius Caesar*, in which he also acted. The influence of English teacher Andrew Davis developed Jarman's love of English literature.

1960 Jarman was offered a place at the Slade School of Art at London University. His father was not happy that he should study art, but agreed to finance his art school training if he first studied for a straightforward university degree. Jarman began a BA at King's College, London in English, History and History of Art. He was involved with the student drama group, designing shows and posters and generally helping backstage. He was also art editor of the student magazine *Lucifer* in his second and third years. In one edition Jarman was described as follows: '2nd Year General Arts. Hopes to paint. Likes Portobello and Caledonian, Wren churches and Stilton.

Above: Jarman on his first birthday

OPPOSITE Jarman at the final mix of *Blue*, 1993. A long-time admirer of Yves Klein, whose monochrome blue canvases inspired the film, Jarman wrote of him in *Chroma* as 'the great master of blue.... No other painter is commanded by blue.'

161

Dislikes the Shell building and all those who disagree.'

Jarman was introduced to American poetry of the 'Beat Generation' (Kerouac, Corso, Ginsberg, Ferlinghetti and Burroughs) by Eric Mottram, the poet, editor and critic, who was on the staff at King's.

Jarman's interest in architecture had been fostered by Robin Noscoe, the art master at Canford, who designed his own house (now complete with a study door painted with text and decoration by Jarman) while Jarman was at Canford. This architectural awareness was developed further under the guidance of Nikolaus Pevsner, whose lectures at London University Jarman attended in the course of his history of art studies.

Jarman arranged to attend drawing classes at the Slade whilst at King's.

1961 Jarman was joint winner in the amateur category of the University of London Union/*Daily Express* art exhibition (David Hockney won the professional category).

1962 First visits to France, Greece and Switzerland.

1963 Jarman moved from his parents' home in Northwood to a flat in Whitley Court, Coram Street, London.

Jarman obtained an upper second degree from King's and took up a place at the Slade School of Art to study painting with stage design as his second subject. Jarman found the theatre room at the Slade a sympathetic place. (It was here that he produced his 'Tentative ideas for a manifesto after $1\frac{1}{3}$ years at an art school' – see p. 1.)

1964 During his vacations from the Slade Jarman created a stand for children's books for Methuen. First visit to North America.

In September Jarman moved to Priory Road in Camden, London.

1965 Jarman experimented with silkscreens and etchings at the Slade but did not pursue

The poem 'Christmas 1964' from Notebook G3, later published in *A Finger in the Fishes Mouth*

print-making to any extent (only a handful of prints are known). Discussions with a theology student, Roger Jones, contributed to his adopting a more open attitude to his homosexuality which was certainly easier to sustain at the Slade than at Kings.

During the vacation Jarman taught English to foreign students. He also set up a short-lived business with Lawrence Warwick-Evans buying, restoring and decorating second-hand furniture.

1966 Moved to Liverpool Road, London.

1967 Designed shop interiors for About Face boutiques in Balham and Streatham jointly with Peter Doherty. The new shops, run by Keith Dodge, who had worked with John Stevens in Carnaby Street, did not prove a success. According to Peter Doherty, the abstract designs were more likely to drive people out of the shop than encourage them to stay in and buy clothes.

Jarman was included in the opening show of the Lisson Gallery, established by a fellow Slade student, Nicholas Logsdail. Further shows followed later in 1967, 1969 and 1970.

Jarman obtained his Diploma in Fine Art at the Slade and almost immediately exhibited in a number of prestigious exhibitions including the *Young Contemporaries* at the Tate Gallery and John Moore's Exhibition in Liverpool. He was also selected for both the Edinburgh *Open 100* and the Fifth Biennale des Jeunes Artistes in Paris, where he exhibited designs for Prokofiev's ballet *The Prodigal Son*. He turned away from the blandishments of Pop art and the figure-based work of David Hockney and developed an increasingly sparing and austere approach to landscape, combining increasingly empty desert scenes, pyramids, fire, distant mountain ranges, dolmens and megaliths.

Exhibitions (* indicates one-man show)
1958–60 Canford School, Dorset

1960 True Lovers' Knot Pub, Northwood*
1961 University of London and *Daily Express* Art Exhibition (joint amateur winner); Watford Central Library;* art by students at schools in the Poole area
1961–62 Bethnal Green Mission, London
1966 Rimmel Gallery, London*
1967 *Young Contemporaries*, Tate Gallery, London (prizewinner); Edinburgh *Open 100*; Lisson Gallery, London (twice); John Moore's Exhibition, Liverpool; Fifth Biennale des Jeunes Artistes, Musée d'Art Moderne, Paris

Stage design
1960 *Julius Caesar* (Canford School)
1962 *The Crucible, The Pillars of the Community* (King's College)
1964 *Measure for Measure* (Slade project)
1965 *Orpheus* (Slade project)
1966 *Volpone, Lt Kije, Coppelia, Huis Clos, Timon of Athens, The Prodigal Son* (Slade projects); *La Ronde* (London Drama Centre)

Jarman with *Cool Waters* at *Young Contemporaries at the Tate*, 1967

1968–76

1968 Shortly after leaving the Slade, Jarman was chosen by Frederick Ashton to design *Jazz Calendar*, a new ballet that Ashton was choreographing to music by Richard Rodney Bennett for the Royal Ballet at Covent Garden in London. He was then asked to design John Gielgud's production of Mozart's *Don Giovanni*, which opened in the English National Opera's new home at the London Coliseum. This was not well received (although the criticism was directed more at Gielgud than at Jarman) and it was over ten years before Jarman again designed an opera.

Jarman was asked to design the ill-fated *Throughway* for Ballet Rambert. The young choreographer Steve Popescu committed suicide after the piece was badly received.

1969 In August he became one of the first artists to move into a Thameside studio in old industrial premises. Other artists with studios at 51 Upper Ground included Peter Logan.

Designed *Poet of Anemones* by Peter Tegel for the Royal Court Theatre.

1970 Jarman moved to 13 Bankside, where other artists with studios included Peter Logan and Michael Ginsberg.

Jarman had his last exhibition at the Lisson Gallery. He also exhibited at the Panegyris Gallery in Copenhagen.

A chance encounter with a stranger on a train led Jarman to meet Ken Russell who asked him to design the set for his forthcoming film, *The Devils*, based on John Whiting's play and on Aldous Huxley's book, *The Devils of Loudon*. Jarman created a stark, dominating, towering white metropolis.

Jarman produced his first 8 mm film, *Studio Bankside*. Jarman made more than a dozen significant Super 8 films between 1970 and 1977. These films, which provided an apprenticeship for his features, like his later

Jarman in his studio in Bankside on the River Thames, 1971

cinema films, display the same interests and concerns as his painting and stage design – landscape (there are practically no figure paintings), megalithic cultures, alchemy and ancient Egypt, English literature, *The Tempest* in particular, the work of Paul Nash, fire, light, water and deserts.

During the 1970s Jarman wrote a series of film scripts of which only some were realized (he wrote or significantly revised almost all the scripts for his films).

His first visit to Italy and memories of earlier visits to Greece resulted in a series of canvases creating abstract designs from fragmentary statue and ceramics remains. Neither capriccios nor still lifes, these abstract studies show both the formal and the decorative aspect of Jarman's work.

1972 Publication of his first book, a collection of poems, *A Finger in the Fishes Mouth*.

The success of his set for *The Devils* led to a further design commission from Russell, for *Savage Messiah*, the story of the sculptor Henri Gaudier and his relationship with Sophie Brzeska. The recreation of turn-of-the-century London and the Vorticist and Omega Workshop movements gave Jarman different sorts of problems: how to create a great deal of sculpture and painted furniture in a short space of time. The problems were overcome with practical help from a team of young artists including Tony Cragg, Bill Woodrow and Christopher Hobbs. Later collaborations with Russell were to come to nothing. Plans to design Russell's production of Peter Maxwell Davies's opera *Taverner* at Covent Garden later that year fell through.

1973 Russell's *Gargantua*, a film for which Jarman produced a number of drawings, foundered for lack of finance.

In May Jarman moved to another warehouse on the banks of the Thames, at Butler's Wharf.

In the early 1970s Jarman's sister Gaye and her husband, David Temple, bought The Verzons, a restaurant just outside Hereford, with a view to turning it into a hotel. Jarman

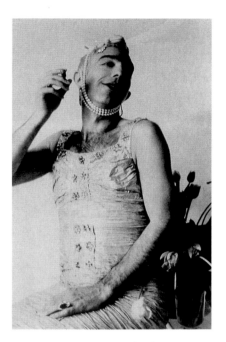

Jarman as Miss Crepe Suzette, London, 1975

designed a garden for them, and work started on implementing his plan, but The Verzons was sold before it was completed. Nothing significant now remains of Jarman's designs except for drawings, and two classical busts created for the garden by Christopher Hobbs.

Jarman returned to ballet with designs for London Festival Ballet's *Silver Apples of the Moon*, choreographed by Tim Spain with music by Morton Subotnik.

1974 Jarman designed two *pas de deux* for a Ballet Gala for the Friends of Fatherless Families, presented by stars from the Royal Ballet at the London Palladium. Only one of the pieces was presented due to injury.

1975 Having come third as Mrs Hippy at the first competition in 1973, Jarman won first prize as Miss Crepe Suzette in the 3rd Alternative Miss World Competition organized by Andrew Logan. His prize was a sculpted leg

Gerald Incandela on location, *Sebastiane,* 1976

made by Andrew Logan, once complete with garter (since lost).

1976 Jarman's first full-length feature film, *Sebastiane,* released. Made in Sardinia, it tells an unconventional version, in Latin, of the story of the martyrdom of St Sebastiane, the captain of Emperor Diocletian's palace guard. The film critic Tony Rayns has said that 'he approached film as a painter rather than a story teller and his films are perhaps best watched with an eye for the magic of image and composition.'

Jarman exhibited at a group show celebrating the Bicentenary of American Independence in Houston, Texas.

Exhibitions (* indicates one-man show)
1969 Lisson Gallery, London;* *The English Landscape Tradition in the Twentieth Century,* Camden Arts Centre, London
1970 Panegyris Gallery, Copenhagen; Lisson Gallery, London
1971 13 Bankside, London (studio show)
1972 *Drawing,* Museum of Modern Art, Oxford
1973 Warehouse A, Butler's Wharf, London
1976 American Bicentenary Exhibition, De Bose Gallery, Houston, Texas

Stage and film design
1968 Set and costumes for: *Jazz Calendar,* Royal Opera House, London; *Don Giovanni,* Coliseum; *Throughway,* Ballet Rambert, London. Unrealized designs for *Ballet for Small Spaces,* New Arts Centre, London

1969 Set and costumes for *Poet of Anemones,* Royal Court Theatre Upstairs, London; designs for *The Beach,* Collegiate Theatre, London (with Yolanda Sonnabend), *4 Minds,* Drill Hall, London and for cabaret, Peter Logan's studio, London; unrealized designs for *The Dreamers* and *The Tempest*
1970 Set for *The Devils; Midsummer Night's Dream* (unrealized)
1972 *Savage Messiah; Taverner* (unrealized)
1973 *Silver Apples of the Moon* (London Festival Ballet); *Gargantua* (unrealized)
1974 Gala for the Friends of Fatherless Families, London Palladium

Films
1970 *Studio Bankside*
1971–72 *Miss Gaby; A Journey to Avebury*
1972 *A Garden in Luxor; Andrew Logan Kisses the Glitterati*
1973 *The Art of Mirrors; Tarot; In the Shadow of the Sun* (completed 1980)
1974 *The Devils at the Elgin; Fire Island*
1974–75 *Ula's Fête; Duggie Fields*
1974–76 *Sloane Square*
1975 *Corfe Film/Troubadour; Sebastiane Wrap; Gerald's Film; Picnic at Rae's*
1976 *Houston, Texas; Sebastiane*

Jarman (right) interviews Andrew Logan, *c.* 1975

1977–86

1978 Film-making took up more and more of Jarman's time and effort. *Jubilee*, with pop stars Toyah Wilcox and Adam Ant, and Jordan, a leading figure in the punk movement, presents life in late twentieth-century England alongside the perceptions and expectations of Elizabeth I, Ariel and alchemist John Dee.

1979 Jarman's interest in *The Tempest*, John Dee, Elizabethan alchemy and the hermetic tradition combined again in his own version of Shakespeare's play. With the move to full-length feature films his attention switched from painting to cinema. Despite Jarman's own suggestions that he stopped painting when he turned to films, he did continue to paint, although perhaps not so often or so prolifically, and to design for the stage and film (he designed many of his early films himself).

It appears that he acquired books by several writers who were important to him during this period and many more on other subjects of interest to him – Egyptian history and religion, William Blake, James Hillman, the unconventional psychologist and Jungian psychiatrist, Carl Jung himself, alchemy, the hermetic tradition and Dr John Dee.

Jarman made a film of three songs with Marianne Faithfull, *Broken English*.

Jarman moved to his final London address, Phoenix House, Charing Cross Road, just over the road from St Martin's School of Art and around the corner from Maison Bertaux, his regular spot for breakfast and coffee.

1980–82 Jarman designed for Tom Jobes's *One* at the London Contemporary Dance Theatre and Jonathan Gems's *The Secret of the Universe* at the Institute of Contemporary Arts.

1980 Jarman made his first 'black painting'.

He designed the set and costumes for a major opera production in Florence directed by Ken Russell, Stravinsky's *The Rake's Progress*. Russell and Jarman decided to set opera in modern England; Jarman's designs included

sets of Piccadilly Circus and the Angel underground station. Some of his costumes drew their inspiration from punks, new romantics and fetish fashion of the time. Having used gold leaf on the set in Florence, he brought some back with him and started using it in his paintings.

1982 Jarman's show at the Edward Totah Gallery exhibited paintings in which he had scratched through a layer of black paint to reveal the gold underneath (both gold leaf and paint). He then started painting in black and gold, sometimes adding red. Jarman commented, 'I have broken the stranglehold of my landscapes. They had become tedious'.

1984 Jarman published his first volume of autobiographical writings, *Dancing Ledge*, which combines artistic insights and social commentary with confessional fragments and witty reminiscences.

At a significant retrospective exhibition at the ICA in London, Jarman showed over thirty new paintings, developing the work he had exhibited in 1982 at the Edward Totah Gallery. An increasing concern with propagandist, political and social commentary can be seen in all aspects of his work, most strikingly in the series of six large *GBH* paintings. Jarman portrayed a Britain overwhelmed by the forces of repression and conservatism, the break up of the fabric of civil society under the Thatcher government and the apocalyptic engulfing of Britain by fire. It is this vision which was to emerge in his film *The Last of England* (1987).

Jarman started two shorter, lyrical film works: *Imagining October*, about revolution, politics, censorship and artistic activity, made after a visit to the USSR as a guest of Soviet film-makers, and *Angelic Conversation*, in which Shakespeare's sonnets are presented from a homosexual perspective.

Norman Coates, Mark Prizeman, Carlos Villanueva, Melanie Sainsbury and Cristina Norton, known together as NATO (Narrative Architecture Today), designed a house for Jarman in the *Starchoice* exhibition at the Royal

Institute of British Architects in London.

1985 Designed Micha Bergese's *Mouth of the Night* for Mantis Dance Company, London.

1986 After years spent attempting to raise the funds and rewriting the script Jarman finally completed his film about the life of the painter Michelangelo Merisi da Caravaggio. He claimed that the film was one of a limited number that gave a realistic idea of how artists work.

The link between film and visual arts is relevant to Jarman's interest in Caravaggio's art. 'Film is the wedding of light and matter – an alchemical conjunction.' He commented that if Caravaggio was reincarnated today it would be as a film-maker: 'Caravaggio would toss his brushes into the Tiber and pick up Sony's latest video [camera], as painting has degenerated into an obscure hermetic practice, performed by initiates behind closed doors. There is a remarkable lack of emotional force in modern painting. Who could shed a tear for it now? But you can weep at Pasolini's *Gospel According to St Matthew*' (*Dancing Ledge* pp. 9–10).

Jarman played the part of Patrick Procktor in Stephen Frears's film about Joe Orton, *Prick Up Your Ears*. (Other films in which he appeared include *A Bigger Splash*, Jack Hazan's 1973 film about David Hockney; *Night Hawks*, Ron Peck 1978; *Dead Cat*, Dave Lewis 1989; and two RCA student films: as Pasolini in Julian Cole's *Ostia* and the lead role in Alexis Bisticas's *The Clearing*. He also appeared in several of his own films.)

Jarman was nominated for the Turner Prize in recognition of the outstanding visual quality of his films, in particular *Sebastiane*, *Jubilee*, *The Tempest* and *Caravaggio*. At the Turner Prize exhibition he showed 'The Caravaggio Suite'. These nine works utilize black paint and tar with applied objects in the style that he had developed shortly before he began work on the film; several incorporate objects from the film (a knife, a skull, candles and a TV remote control).

On 22 December Jarman was diagnosed HIV positive. Before the diagnosis Jarman's sexuality had been one among a number of significant influences and interests informing his art. After the diagnosis it became the principal, determining factor in his work.

Exhibitions (* indicates one-man show)
1978 Sarah Bradley's Gallery, London*
1981 B2 Gallery, London
1982 Edward Totah Gallery, London*
1984 ICA, London;* *Masks*, Café Gallery, London; International Contemporary Art Fair, London
1986 Turner Prize Exhibition, Tate Gallery, London

Stage design
1980 *One*, London Contemporary Dance Theatre; *The Secret of the Universe*, Institute of Contemporary Arts, London
1982 *The Rake's Progress*, Pergola Theatre, Florence
1983 Zandra Rhodes Fashion Spectacular, London
1985 *Mouth of the Night*, Mantis Dance Company, London

Films
1977 *Jordan's Dance*; *Every Woman for Herself and All for Art*
1978 *Jubilee*; *The Pantheon*
1979 *Broken English* (Marianne Faithfull); *The Tempest*
1980 *T G Psychic Rally in Heaven*
1981 *Jordan's Wedding*
1982 *Ken's First Film*; *Pirate Tape*; *Pontormo Punks at Santa Croce*
1982–83 *Waiting for Waiting for Godot*
1983 Music videos for Carmel, Steve Hale, Wang Chung, Lords of the New Church, Jimmy the Hoover and Billy Hyena
1983–84 *The Dream Machine*
1984 *Imagining October*; Catalan; music videos for Marc Almond and Orange Juice
1985 *Angelic Conversation*; music video for Brian Ferry
1986 Music videos for the Smiths and Easterhouse
1986 *Caravaggio*

1987–95

1987 Jarman had his first solo show with Richard Salmon who remained his dealer until Jarman's death in 1994.

In May, following the death of his father, Jarman bought Prospect Cottage, a wooden fisherman's cottage at Dungeness on the Kent coast, using the proceeds of his father's will. The garden that Jarman created at Prospect Cottage combines plants from the local habitat and the herbals in his collection with flotsam and jetsam from the beach, arranged as sculptures and patterns created out of the pebbles and stones found nearby.

The move to the south coast led directly to a new series of works. Jarman started creating assemblages of objets trouvés which introduced a three-dimensional element into his work for the first time in many years. 'I have been making a whole series of objects out of things that have been thrown up by the sea. There are, of course, fantastic stones on the beach and these have been incorporated into [works] as well as wood.' The black and gold canvases turned to works coated in pitch (or tar or bitumen), into which glass and mirrors were placed and then smashed. He also used a wide range of objets trouvés, knick-knacks, toys, bric-à-brac, flotsam and jetsam, often held in position by the binding power of the pitch, which slowly hardens once applied.

The resulting constructions often make sharp comments on society, politics and gay concerns through their juxtapositions and combinations (the church, social mores, the political scenes and the consumer society were all attacked with the Incredible Hulk, condoms, cheap religious imagery and calculators).

Jarman began to devote a great deal of time and energy to sexual politics. He took part in demonstrations and consolidated his position as a guru and icon, not only for gays around the world but also for young people generally because of his unconventional approach to life and his political opposition to the conservative governments in Britain and other countries.

1988 Jarman directed his first major stage work, Sylvano Bussotti's opera, *L'Ispirazione*, at the Teatro Communale in Florence. Bussotti, one of Italy's major composers, designed the production himself (and incorporated a short film sequence by Jarman).

1989 Jarman acted as concert director and designer for the Pet Shop Boys' tour of Hong Kong and Great Britain.

1990 Jarman made *The Garden*. The basis of the film is provided by home movies Jarman made of his garden, in the shadow of a nuclear power station, with further sequences improvised around the theme of the Gospels.

In January Jarman saw a particularly fine painting of an urban London scene by Frank Auerbach. This encouraged him to paint rather than produce collages and assemblages. The result was many rich, vibrant landscapes, with thickly applied impasto – some are views of Dungeness, others landscapes inspired by the marshland around his home.

The rich impasto came partly no doubt from an aesthetic imperative but also from a deterioration in Jarman's sight, one side effect of his medication. This gradual loss of sight, which was later reversed unexpectedly, is also directly commented on, as are other aspects of his medical struggles, in other paintings.

Jarman with Neil Tennant, projection for the Pet Shop Boys, 1989

Prospect Cottage shortly after Jarman moved in, 1987

1991 Publication of *Modern Nature*, another autobiographical journal.

The Garden was chosen by the International Catholic Organisation for Cinema for Special Mention at the Berlin Film Festival.

Jarman designed Les Blair's production of *Waiting for Godot*, with Rik Mayall and Adrian Edmondson, in London's West End.

On 22 September Jarman was canonized by the Sisters of Perpetual Indulgence as 'St Derek of Dungeness of the Order of Celluloid Knights'.

1992 Publication of *At Your Own Risk*, his book about being gay, AIDS and the way it was treated in the media.

The 'Queer' works were shown at the Manchester City Art Gallery, then Rome and Potsdam. They were largely concerned with the tabloid press's homophobia and were painted over photocopies of newspaper headlines. Later works became increasingly self-referential, documenting his increasing ill health and the onset of AIDS and its related illnesses. His black paintings, pitch constructions and large canvases drew on the paraphernalia of hospitals and treatment (X-rays, blood bags, thermometers, medication, etc.) and the physiological effect of his illnesses upon his body. At the same time his works show a large element of humour and black comedy.

1993 *Blue* was premiered at the Venice Film Festival. It consists of a blue screen with a text and music sound-track. There are no other images. Jarman was particularly interested in the work of Yves Klein ('the great master of blue'). The film is largely about Jarman's state of mind as he underwent treatment for the many AIDS-related illnesses that he suffered from; in particular it is a response to the way his sight was under attack. His script also contains his own moving writing about the loss of many friends and acquaintances. *Blue* was awarded the Michael Powell Prize at the Edinburgh Film Festival.

Jarman was created a Fellow of the Royal College of Art.

Despite increasing ill health Jarman played a significant role in the creation of *Glitterbug*, a compilation of his home movies and earlier Super 8 films, commissioned by the BBC.

Jarman designed Genet's *The Maids* for Maison Bertaux Theatre. It was premiered at the Edinburgh Festival Fringe and then transferred to the London nightclub Heaven.

1994 Publication of *Chroma*, his book on colour. It also contains a version of the script of *Blue*.

After a long series of painful illnesses, Derek Jarman died on 19 February.

1995 Publication of *Derek Jarman's Garden*, which documents the creation of his extraordinary garden at Dungeness.

Exhibitions (* indicates one-man show)
1987 Herbert F. Johnson Museum of Art, Cornell University, New York; Richard Salmon Ltd., London*
1988 Dom Kulture, Studenski Grad, Belgrade*
1989 Richard Salmon Ltd., London;* Accatone, Paris;* Galeria Ambit, Barcelona;* National Review of Live Art, Glasgow; Lyth Arts Centre, Wick, Caithness; Richard Demarco, Edinburgh;* Lydd Airport and Dymchurch Martello Tower, Kent
1990 Terada Warehouse Space T33, Tokyo;* *Self-portraits*, Café Gallery, London
1991 *Edward II*, Carnegie Museum; *Designing Yourself?*, Design Museum, London*
1992 Art Gallery and Museum, Glasgow;* Manchester City Art Gallery;* Karsten Schubert Ltd., London*
1993 Palazzo delle Esposizione, Rome;* Filmmuseum, Potsdam;* Newlyn Art Gallery, Penzance, Cornwall;* The Marsh Gallery, New Romney, Kent;* *From Diaghilev to the Pet Shop Boys*, Central St Martin's School of Art and Design, London
1994 Chesil Gallery, Portland, Dorset;* Whitworth Art Gallery, Manchester;* Drew Gallery, Canterbury, Kent*

1994–95 *New Painting*, Arts Council of Great Britain Touring Exhibition
1996 Barbican Art Gallery, London;* Hatton Gallery, Newcastle upon Tyne;* Sainsbury Centre, Norwich*; *The Hall of Mirrors*, Museum of Contemporary Art, Los Angeles

Stage design
1991 Designed *Waiting for Godot* with Madeleine Morris, Queen's Theatre, London
1992 Designed *The Maids* with Nicole Robinson, Maison Bertaux Theatre, London

Films
1987 *Aria*; *The Last of England*; music videos for Bob Geldof, the Pet Shop Boys and the Mighty Lemon Drops
1989 *War Requiem*
1990 *The Garden*
1991 *Edward II*
1992 *Wittgenstein*
1993 *Blue*; *Glitterbug*; music videos for Patti Smith and Suede

Collecting stones on the beach, New Year's Day 1993

Bibliography

By Derek Jarman

'The Linear Quality of English Art', *Lucifer* magazine, King's College, London (Lent 1962)

'Notes found on the body of a BA student', *Lucifer* magazine, King's College, London (Lent 1963)

A Finger in the Fishes Mouth (poems), Bettiscombe Press, Bettiscombe, Dorset 1972

Dancing Ledge, Quartet, London 1984

Caravaggio, Thames and Hudson, London 1986

The Last of England, Constable, London 1987

War Requiem, Faber and Faber, London 1989

Modern Nature, Century, London 1991

Today and Tomorrow, Richard Salmon, London 1991

Queer Edward II, BFI Publishing, London 1991

At Your Own Risk: A Saint's Testament, Hutchinson, London 1992

Wittgenstein, BFI Publishing, London 1993

Blue, BFI Publishing, London/Overlook, NY 1993

Chroma, Century, London 1994

Blue (limited edition film script, 150 with original blue silkscreen by Jarman, 25 *de tête* with leather binding and original painting by Jarman on the cover), Salmon Shaw Dane Watson, London 1994

Derek Jarman's Garden, Thames and Hudson, London 1995

Up in the Air: Derek Jarman's Collected Film Scripts, includes: *Akhenaten* (unrealized), 1975; *Jubilee*, 1978; *Neutron* (unrealized), 1979–83; *B Movie: Little England/A Time of Hope*, 1981; *Bob Up and Down* (unrealized), 1981–84; *Sodem* (unrealized, undated)

Kicking the Pricks (retitled paperback edition of *The Last of England*), Vintage, London 1996

Unpublished work by Derek Jarman

The Quest for Geoge Daly (drama fragment), 1964

The Picnic and other drama fragments, 1964

Through the Billboard Promised Land (unrealized script), 1965

Decadence (unrealized script), 1972–75

Little England (unrealized script), 1972–75

In the Shadow (unrealized script), 1972–75

Green Glass Bead/Fire (unrealized script), 1972–75

The PT Lessons of Eva Braun (unrealized script), 1974

Kingdom of Outremer/Kingdom Over the Sea (unrealized script), 1974

Bible Story (unrealized script, with Ken Russell), 1974

Summoning of Angels (unrealized script), 1975

John Dee (unrealized script), 1975

Glass Film/Breaking Glass (unrealized script), 1975

Sands of Time (unrealized script), 1975

Archaeologies/Notes for Archaeology of Sound (unrealized script), 1975–78

Nijinsky's Last Hope (unrealized script), 1984

Lossiemouth (unrealized script), 1985

On Derek Jarman

'Derek Jarman… Of Angels and Apocalypse', *Afterimage* No. 12, autumn 1985

The Complete Derek Jarman (exhibition catalogue), Stuttgart 1988

Frieze Frame (film stills), Uplink, Tokyo 1993

Ian Lucas, *Impertinent Decorum*, Cassell, London 1994

Matthew D. Cook, *Derek Jarman: reclaiming the past, writing the future* (unpublished MA thesis, Queen Mary and Westfield College, London University), 1994

Visueller Sound: Musikvideos zwischen Avantgarde und Populärkultur, eds. C. Hauser and A Schonholzer, Zyklop Verlag, Lucerne 1994

Gaia Shaw, *Queer Gravity: Alchemy and sexuality in Derek Jarman's films and paintings* (unpublished MA dissertation, Wimbledon School of Art and University of Surrey), 1994

Maggie Taylor, *Jarman's Gentle Joke: An examination of the use of irony in Derek Jarman's The Tempest* (unpublished MA thesis, University of Auckland, New Zealand), 1994

Michael O'Pray, *Derek Jarman: Dreams of England*, BFI Publishing, London 1996

Broadcasts

'South of Watford', ITV, 1984

'Know what I mean' (directed by Laurens C. Postma), a Yo Yo Film Production for Channel 4, 1988

'In the Psychiatrist's Chair', Jarman in conversation with Anthony Clare, BBC Radio, 1990

'Derek Jarman: a portrait' (directed by Mark Kidel), Arena, BBC Television, 1991

'Building Sights' (directed by Keith Collins), Jarman at Robin Noscoe's Garden House, Wimborne Minster, BBC Television, 1991

'There we are John' (directed by Ken McMullen), British Council, 1993

'Face to Face', Jarman in conversation with Jeremy Isaacs, BBC Television, 1993

Sources of illustrations

Note: all photographs credited to Prudence Cuming Associates and A. C. Cooper Ltd. are copyright and reproduced by courtesy of Richard Salmon Ltd., London. All works owned by the Estate of Derek Jarman reproduced by courtesy of the Estate.

Jacket: *front* photo © Howard Sooley (1992); *back, clockwise from top left* photos © Howard Sooley (1993), Ray Dean (1968), Howard Sooley (1992), Mike Laye (1987)

Endpapers Drawings for 'Corfe Castle' film from Film Projects Notebook A1, Sloane Square, 1975. Collection: Keith Collins. Photograph: Rik Walton

1 From Notebook G3 ('A British Gallery of Pictures III', winter 1964). Collection: Keith Collins. Photograph: Rik Walton
2 Jarman after completing *Dead Sexy*, May 1993. Photograph: Howard Sooley
4 Jarman priming canvases, 1992. Photograph: Howard Sooley
5 From Notebook C3C, September 1973. Collection: Keith Collins. Photograph: Rik Walton
6 From Notebook A2, March 1975. Collection: Keith Collins. Photograph: Rik Walton
8, 9 Photograph: John Dewe-Matthews
10 Above left: photograph: Liam Longman. Reproduced by courtesy of Basilisk Communications; below left, centre right, below right, collection: Keith Collins. Photographs: Rik Walton
11 Photograph: Howard Sooley
12 Present whereabouts unknown. Photograph: Ray Dean
13 Photograph: Gordon Rainsford
14 Present whereabouts unknown. Photograph: Ray Dean
16 Above, collection: Keith Collins. Photograph: Rik Walton; below, private collection. Photograph: Fraser Marr
17 Untitled drawing, 30 x 22 in. (76.2 x 55.9 cm). Private collection. Photograph: Fraser Marr
19 Photograph: Ray Dean
20 Private collection. Photograph: Fraser Marr
21 Photograph: Ray Dean
22 *The Equivalents for the Megaliths*, 26 x 18 in. (66 x 45.7 cm). Collection: Tate Gallery, London. Reproduced by courtesy of the Tate Gallery and with the permission of the Paul Nash Trust
23 *Archeologies*, 7.5 x 5.4 in. (19 x 13.75 cm). Private collection. Photograph: Fraser Marr
24 Top row, left to right: untitled (candle), *Nightlife*, untitled (crucifix), *The World's Last Night*, untitled (candle and sleep). Middle row, left to right: *Blue Is Poison*, untitled (channel changer), *Perfect Moment 1*. Bottom: *The Knife*. Dimensions between 12 x 16 in. (31 x 41 cm) and 18 x 16 in. (46 x 41 cm). Estate of Derek Jarman. Photograph: Prudence Cuming Associates
25 *The Inheritance*, 10 x 12 in. (25.5 x 30.5 cm). Private collection. Photograph: Prudence Cuming Associates; *The Instruments of Her Passion*, 14 x 30 in. (35.6 x 76.2 cm). Private collection. Photograph: Prudence Cuming Associates
28 Above, photograph: Foto Marchiori; below, photograph: Guy Gravett. Reproduction by courtesy of Glyndebourne Festival Opera
32 Photograph: Howard Sooley
36 Photograph: Alistair Thain. Reproduced by courtesy of BFI Production and Basilisk Communications
39 Photograph: Mike Laye. Reproduced by courtesy of Basilisk Communications
41 Photograph: Mike Laye
42 Collection: Keith Collins. Photograph: Rik Walton
45 Photograph reproduced by courtesy of Basilisk Communications
49 *Self-Portrait*, 25 x 30 in. (63.5 x 76.2 cm), private collection. Photograph: Fraser Marr
50 *2nd Potters Bar Fête*, 22 x 18 in. (55.9 x 45.7 cm). Private collection. Photographs: Fraser Marr
51 *We Wait and Wait*, 19 x 24 in. (48.3 x 70 cm). Private collection. Photograph: Fraser Marr

52, 53 Present whereabouts unknown.
Photographs: Ray Dean

54 *Sculpture Garden*, 84 x 69 in.
(213.4 x 175.3 cm). Present whereabouts
unknown. Photographs: Ray Dean

55 *Pleasures of Italy 2*, 88 x 65 in.
(223.5 x 165.1 cm); *From Poussin's Inspiration
of a Poet*. Both private collections.
Photographs: Fraser Marr

56 Above, present whereabouts unknown.
Photograph: Ray Dean; untitled, 9 x 7 in.
(22.25 x 17.75 cm), private collection.
Photograph: Fraser Marr

57 *Cool Waters*, 96 ½ x 72 ¼ in. (245 x 183.5 cm).
The work was sold but the purchaser
found it was too large and Jarman painted
a slightly smaller version (present
whereabouts unknown). Jarman gave
the original to a friend, the photographer
Ray Dean. Collection and photograph:
Ray Dean

58 Avebury Series No. 4, 48 x 48 in.
(122 x 122 cm). Collection and
photograph: Northampton Art Gallery.
Sand Base, 21 x 19 in. (53.3 x 48.3 cm).
Photograph: Roger Wollen

59 Untitled landscape, 48 x 48 in.
(122 x 122 cm). Private collection.
Photograph: Fraser Marr

60 'A garden for The Verzons', 10 x 4 ½ in.
(25.4 x 11.4 cm). Private collection.
Photograph: Fraser Marr. Top right and
left, collection: Keith Collins; Photographs:
Rik Walton. Centre right, private collection.
Photograph: Fraser Marr

61 Top and centre, present whereabouts
unknown. Photographs: Ray Dean; below,
collection: Keith Collins. Photograph:
Rik Walton

62, 63 *Irresistible Grace*, 54 x 72 in. (137.25
x 183 cm). *Untitled (Archer)*, 14 x 18 in.
(35.5 x 46.25 cm). Estate of Derek Jarman.
Photographs: Prudence Cuming Associates

64 Photograph: Mike Laye.

66, 67 Photographs: Jean Marc Prouveur,
courtesy British Film Institute Stills,
Posters and Designs

68 Photograph: David Bramley, courtesy

Don Boyd and British Film Institute Stills,
Posters and Designs

70, 71 Photograph: Mike Laye. Reproduced by
courtesy of Basilisk Communications

72 Photograph: Liam Longman. Reproduced
by courtesy of Basilisk Communications

74 Photograph: Liam Longman. Reproduced
courtesy British Film Institute Stills,
Posters and Designs, National Film Trustee
Co. Ltd. and Working Title Films Ltd.

76, 79 Photographs: Bridget Holm

80 Collection: Keith Collins. Photograph:
Rik Walton

82 Present whereabouts of all projects
unknown. Photographs: Ray Dean

83 Above, photograph: Ray Dean; below,
present whereabouts unknown.
Photograph: Ray Dean

84, 85 Photographs: Ray Dean

86, 87 Photographs: Foto Marchiori

89 Above, collection: Royal Opera House.
Reproduced by courtesy of the Royal
Opera House, London; below, photograph:
Ray Dean

90 Above, present whereabouts unknown.
Photograph: Ray Dean; below, 11 x 9 in.
(28 x 22.75 cm), private collection.
Photograph: Fraser Marr

91 Photograph: Ray Dean

92 Present whereabouts of all projects
unknown. Photographs: Ray Dean

93 Photograph: Ray Dean

94 Above left, photograph: Ray Dean;
above right, from Notebook C3C,
September 1973. Collection: Keith Collins.
Photograph: Rik Walton; below,
photograph: Dee Conway

95 Photographs: Nicole Robinson

96 Above, photograph: Ray Dean; below,
collection: Keith Collins. Photograph:
Rik Walton

97 All reproduced by courtesy of James
Mackay

98, 99 Photographs: Bridget Holm

100 Photograph: Mike Laye

101 Photographs: Liam Longman.
Reproduced by courtesy of Basilisk
Communications

102, 103 Photographs: Mike Laye

104 Photograph: Howard Sooley

120, 121 *Scream*, 84 x 84 in. (213.5 x 213.5 cm).
Silence, 16 x 20 in. (40.75 x 50.75 cm).
Estate of Derek Jarman. Photographs:
Prudence Cuming Associates

122 *The Mistake*, 10 x 12 in. (25.4 x 30.5 cm).
Estate of Derek Jarman. Photograph:
Prudence Cuming Associates. *These
Thoughts*, 20 x 20 in. (50.2 x 50.2 cm).
Collection: Lynn Hanke, New York.
Photograph: Prudence Cuming Associates

123 *Prospect – The Shadow Takes on Substance*,
10 x 14 1/2 in. (25.5 x 36.75 cm). TB or
Not TB, 16 x 18 in. (40.6 x 46 cm). Estate
of Derek Jarman. Photographs: Prudence
Cuming Associates

124 Landscape, 84 x 84 in. (213.5 x 213.5 cm).
Estate of Derek Jarman. Photograph:
Pia Goddard

125 Both landscapes, 18 x 16 in.
(45.7 x 40.6 cm). Estate of Derek Jarman.
Photograph: Pia Goddard

126 58 1/4 x 99 in. (149 x 251.5 cm), private
collection. Photograph: Prudence Cuming
Associates

127 Private collection and Estate of Derek
Jarman. Photograph: Prudence Cuming
Associates

128 *Blood*, 70 1/2 x 99 in. (179 x 251.5 cm),
Estate of Derek Jarman. Photograph:
Prudence Cuming Associates

129 Photographs by Howard Sooley

130, 131, 132 *Infection*, 70 1/2 x 99 in.
(179 x 251 cm); *Fuck Me Blind*, 70 1/2 x 99
in. (179 x 251 cm); *Spread the Plague*, 58 1/2 x
99 in. (149 x 251.5 cm), Estate of Derek
Jarman. Photographs: Prudence Cuming
Associates

133, 134 *Do Lalley*, 84 x 84 in.
(213.5 x 213.5 cm); *Dipsy Do (Sinister)*,
84 x 84 in. (213.5 x 213.5 cm); Estate of
Derek Jarman. Photograph: A. C. Cooper
Ltd.

135 *Dizzy Bitch*, 84 x 84 in. (213.5 x 213.5 cm);
Estate of Derek Jarman. Photograph:
Prudence Cuming Associates

136 *Queer*, 70 1/2 x 99 in. (179 x 251 cm).
Collection: Manchester City Art Gallery.
Photograph: Prudence Cuming Associates

141 Photograph: Howard Sooley

142 Photograph: Gordon Rainsford

145 Photograph: Gordon Rainsford

146, 153, 154–55, 156 Photographs: Howard
Sooley

157 *Ego et in Arcadia*, 10 x 10 in
(25.5 x 25.5 cm). Estate of Derek Jarman.
Photograph: Pia Goddard

158–59, 160 Photographs: Liam Longman,
reproduced by courtesy of Basilisk
Communications

161 Jarman on his first birthday

162 Collection: Keith Collins. Photograph:
Rik Walton

163 Collection: Ray Dean. Photograph:
Ray Dean

164 Photograph: Ray Dean

165 Photograph: Marc Balet, reproduced by
courtesy of the photographer

166 Above, photograph: Guy Ford/Bevis
Bowden. Reproduced courtesy of Guy
Ford; below, photograph: John Dewe-
Matthews

169 Photograph: Liam Longman. Reproduced
courtesy of Basilisk Communications

170, 171 Photographs: Howard Sooley

Index

Page numbers in *italic* refer to illustrations

The film can amalgam
of the breaking mirror
structured ghost film *
flashes into the curre

the gatehouse and two
which a figure to see
reveal the castle

* the progressi